MW00378039

VOLUME TWO

Great American Homes

WILLIAM T. BAKER

VOLUME TWO

Great American Homes

WILLIAM T. BAKER

PHOTOGRAPHY BY
JAMES R. LOCKHART

images
Publishing

Published in Australia in 2012 by
The Images Publishing Group Pty Ltd
ABN 89 059 734 431
6 Bastow Place, Mulgrave, Victoria 3170, Australia
Tel: +61 3 9561 5544 Fax: +61 3 9561 4860
books@imagespublishing.com
www.imagespublishing.com

The Images Publishing Group Reference Number: 1031

National Library of Australia Cataloguing-in-Publication entry:

Author:	Baker, William T.
Title:	Great American homes Volume 2 / William T. Baker
ISBN:	9781864704839 (hbk.)
Series:	New classicists
Subjects:	Architecture, Domestic—United States
	Architect-designed houses—United States
Dewey Number:	728

Edited by Driss Fatih

Designed by The Graphic Image Studio Pty Ltd, Mulgrave, Australia
www.tgis.com.au

Pre-publishing services by Mission Productions Limited, Hong Kong
Printed by Paramount Printing Company Limited Hong Kong
on 140gsm Chinese Matt Art

Contents

FOREWORD

In 1945 the renowned eclectic architect David Adler defined his work to be 'all in the period of the great house, which he said [was] alas over.' His oeuvre included Italian Renaissance villas, French chateaux, Georgian, and Federal styles, among many other classic vernaculars. And although Adler was unquestionably prescient in his declaration at the time, his work, and that of many of his contemporaries, inspired a succession of architects and clients who mutually, during the past several decades, have revitalized interest in houses evocative of a bygone era. William T. Baker follows in this long line of distinguished work.

How did first I become familiar with the work of William Baker? When *Southern Accents* was in circulation, I read the magazine regularly, and in one issue, nearly 20 years ago, I was awestruck by a handsome Georgian house that featured in an advertisement for Baker's firm in Atlanta. I wanted to move in immediately!

The Krone House, as the commission is known, resurrects classical Georgian design and materials not found appreciably in Atlanta for more than 70 years. The symmetrical façade of the house, with its Buckingham slate roof, is composed of wood mold brick laid with white mortar in a running bond pattern. The red brick, which is reminiscent of 18th-century fabrication, is handsomely augmented by a central bay clad in Indiana limestone carved by a British artisan and set by a stonemason from New York. Limestone also forms the four full-length Corinthian order pilasters spanning the front of the house, and the segmental and triangular pediments capping the custom mahogany front door and pair of first-floor French doors. During the late 1980s, when the house was built, such stonework in Atlanta was rare. Fortunately, Baker was able to recreate it then for the Krone commission.

The interior plan of Krone House also harmonizes classic and timeless design of the past with casual living of today. Great houses of a century ago were built for formal lifestyles where families gathered only in the living room, library, and dining room. However, in the 21st century, families such as the Krones also gravitate to the keeping room or family room, which as the center of family life today, is incorporated in an open plan with the kitchen and breakfast room, thereby replacing the segregated servants' sitting room and dining room, which were once the norm in a formal way of life.

William Baker's commission for Mr. and Mrs. Krone represents a wide array of houses that he has thoughtfully designed to meet the evolving American floor plan and changing lifestyles without compromising scale, proportion, and inherent classicism. Baker is also responding to the American Dream, a principal aspiration dating back to the early days of the United States, when people had the right and opportunity to work hard, achieve success, and live life without class restrictions and religious constraints ingrained in past societies. It was a world that was unique to America.

However, what coincided with the establishment of the new society was the desire to replicate or seek influence from the great architecture of the past. Churches and synagogues, which incorporated classical detailing, elegant proportions and highly crafted elements, exposed Americans regularly to pedigreed design. Then, as families achieved economic success, they aspired to live in houses reflecting what they had seen and of which they had developed an appreciation.

Affluent Americans also traveled abroad and saw first-hand the great historic architectural styles of domestic and institutional buildings, and explored how they could be applied to their own lifestyles at home. Fortunately, they also had the enrichment of scholars of architecture, such as David Adler and Richard Morris Hunt—the latter one of America's most prolific architects, who went to Paris during the mid-1800s to study at the Ecole des Beaux-Arts, the preeminent school of architecture and design in the world. Hunt, who was also the first American to attend the French institution, brought back to the United States what he learned and cultivated a clientele who wanted to live the American Dream, initially in Newport, the summer enclave of American wealth where ever-growing aspirations for grand living modeled on European royalty were fervent.

Hunt and his contemporaries enabled Americans to reclaim the architecture that they had left behind, albeit with a lifestyle that was comparatively free of restrictions. These architects also correlated the new-found affluence in America with its European counterparts, allowing Americans unbridled access to various architectural styles of which they might otherwise have been deprived, had they and their forebears not settled and flourished in the New World.

Architects in the New World not only followed Europe in its classical language; they also adapted the various styles of the Old World. They designed houses in the English and French vernaculars, which evolved primarily along the Atlantic seaboard, and Mediterranean-inspired architecture, which became appropriate in the more arid Western regions. However, there were also American eclectic architects, such as Adler, who were extremely versatile and replicated a focal range of historic styles without relevance to location, climate, or topography. Along the Gold Coast of Long Island and the North Shore of Chicago, French chateaux, Italian Renaissance villas, and French Normandy models coexist harmoniously and skillfully recreate Old World impressions. Regardless of their situation, they are all perfectly at home in the United States.

While the fashion of grand houses in classical styles ebbs and flows with national tastes, there remains today a demand for such houses among families who still desire to live in classically designed houses. Furthermore, Americans have adjusted to the absence of another hierarchy—the household staff—who were both proud and capable of caring for the great houses. Our modern families have been able to embrace a less formal and pared-down lifestyle and have retained the best from the past and melded it with the reality of present-day

living. They have raised and nurtured their children in these homes, and the plan of these houses will no doubt evolve further as family life continues to change.

Affluent lifestyles have also facilitated another idiom of the American Dream—the vacation house. This dwelling is an extension of the family home and allows Americans the privilege and freedom of another place to nest, grow, and experience an architectural style that differs from their permanent home. Leisure is an important part of the American Dream and the vacation house provides the perfect setting for life at the beach, the lake, or the mountains. Some of Baker's most interesting designs for these types of houses are illustrated in this volume. His use of rustic or natural materials gives these houses a texture and feel that is a surprising contrast to his more well-known classical designs. Whether it his use of native stone, a tree trunk, or tree bark, his ability to weave these together into a successful composition testifies to his talent as a designer of houses that transcend our preconceived definition of the classical house.

William Baker's work clearly reflects the aspirations of the American Dream. His creative talent and discriminating standards for good taste have resulted in architecture that is a celebration of the American Dream. This, along with his astute comprehension of life as it is lived in the 21st century, makes these houses a living testament to all the possibilities of the good life.

Stephen Salny

GEORGIAN GRANDEUR IN ATLANTA

Ferrari/Leebern House, Atlanta, Georgia, 2002

Georgian architecture has always struck a familiar chord with Americans. Perhaps it is our English roots, especially in Georgia, or perhaps it is the colors and textures of the characteristic brick and limestone materials that seem so at home in this environment. Over the past two centuries, Georgian style has been explored and perfected. Today, we can see a classic example in this fine house in Atlanta.

Entering the foyer, one sees the wood staircase with its thick balusters and newel post that hints at the attention to detail lavished upon the interiors. Wainscot paneling and arched openings with fluted pilasters frame the

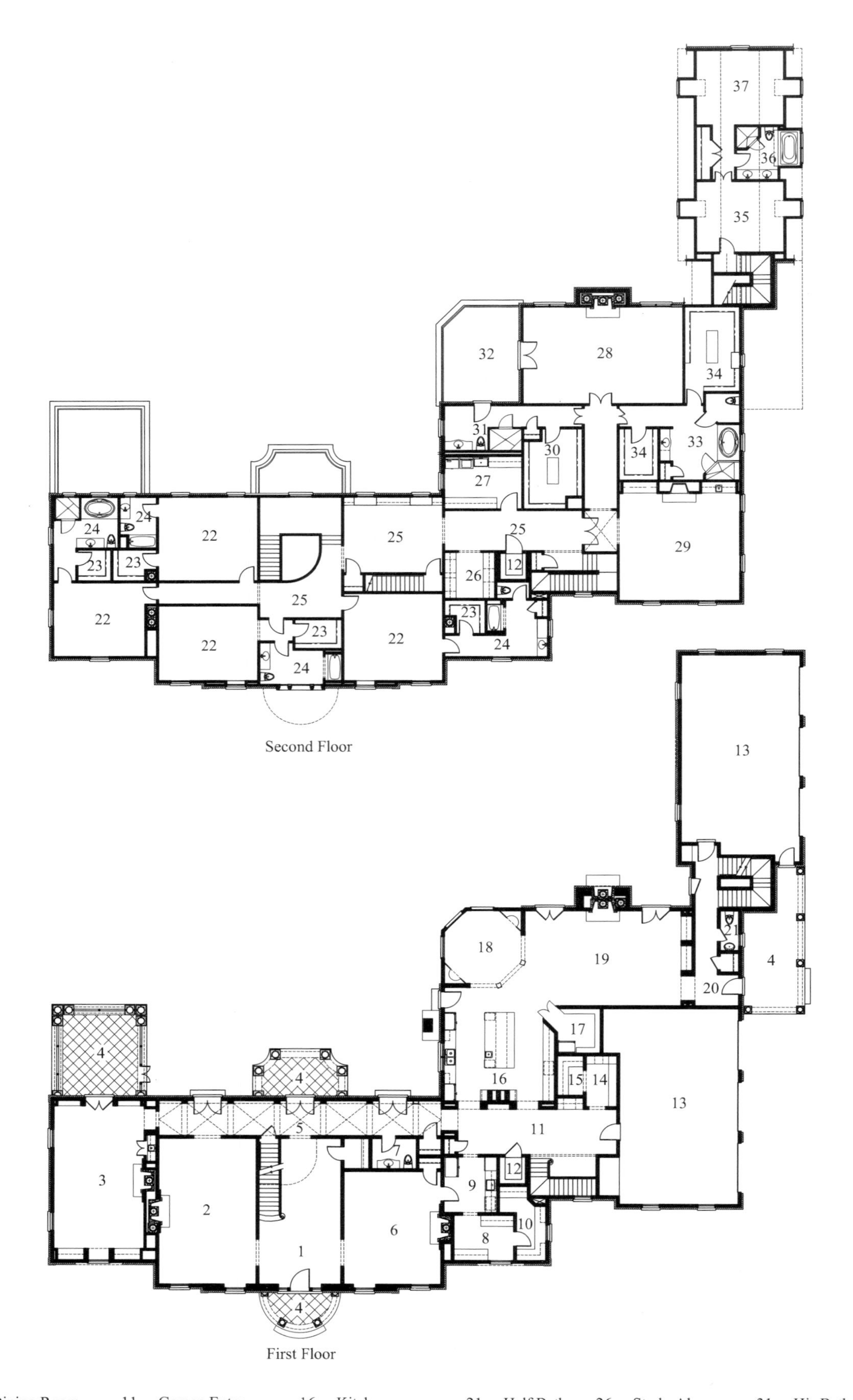

Second Floor

First Floor

1 Foyer
2 Living Room
3 Paneled Study
4 Porch
5 Groin Vault Hall
6 Dining Room
7 Powder Room
8 Butler's Pantry
9 Caterer's Kitchen
10 Pantry
11 Garage Entry
12 Elevator
13 Garage
14 Children's Lockers
15 Office Nook
16 Kitchen
17 Kitchen Pantry
18 Breakfast Room
19 Family Room
20 Rear Entry Hall
21 Half Bath
22 Bedroom
23 Closet
24 Bathroom
25 Stair Hall
26 Study Alcove
27 Laundry
28 Master Bedroom
29 Master Sitting
30 His Closet
31 His Bath
32 Open Terrace
33 Her Bath
34 Her Closet
35 Staff Sitting Room
36 Staff Bath
37 Staff Bedroom

entrances to the adjoining living and dining rooms. The period mantles that adorn these rooms were made in England, and complement the cornices and other trim accenting these principal entertainment rooms.

The plan offers the quiet elegance of an older home, yet provides all the amenities required of a modern family home. The open floor plan of the kitchen, breakfast, and family room area allows the house to exist comfortably, whether entertaining in grand style in the principal rooms, or informally in the rooms opening onto the pool terrace.

Living room mantle

Houses of this type look best centered on a wide sweeping lawn with mature trees framing the lawn and providing scale to the house. The expansive lawn and slightly elevated position on a ridge provide

Library

Groin vault hallway to library

an ideal setting for this house. From this elevated point, one can enjoy a horizon view of the setting sun from the rear terrace. The dense forest of pines and poplar trees to the rear of the house provides a black silhouette against the pink sky of the evening light.

Dining room mantle

Laundry

Kitchen

Her bathroom

Upper stair hall

Breakfast room

Rear elevation

Library porch

Twilight in Georgia

WILLOW OAK FARM

Madison, Georgia, 2001–2002
Interiors by Dan Carithers, Atlanta, Georgia

Country retreats have a long and celebrated history in the South. At one time, these family homesteads were where livelihoods were made from farming and cattle. Over time, many of these properties have transitioned to a new purpose: the family retreat. Used throughout the year for holiday gatherings, weekend or summer getaways, seasonal hunting, and for special events such as a family wedding, these retreats become an important part of cherished memories.

For this southern family, all these events are enjoyed on this expansive property, located in one of the state's most pristine rural counties. Over the years, the family has added to the buildings on the property. The original 19th-century farmhouse now anchors a compound of buildings that were built to meet the needs of multiple generations of this large family.

Screen porch

The most recent addition to the farm is the guest house. A long screen porch across the front of the house provides a shaded place to sit in rocking chairs and pass the time visiting, reading, or just enjoying the view of the garden.

The design of the open floor plan provides casual entertaining space that allows for maximum family interaction. The sitting area, dining areas, and kitchen open as one large space. Yet the spaces are separated

Front door

In Pursuit of Refinement
MADISON: A Classic Southern Town
easy COTTAGE style
The FARMHOUSE
Roots of Home
Art of Celebration
GARDENS OF HISTORIC CHARLESTON
ANNIE KELLY ROOMS TO INSPIRE IN THE COUNTRY
NATIONAL GEOGRAPHIC

Great room

the southern cottage
BUNNY WILLIAMS AN AFFAIR WITH A HOUSE
Cabins & Camps

Dining area

Great room fireplace

Breakfast area

by the clever use of wood timber and post columns that define the spaces without creating visual barriers. The result is a delightful house that is comfortable to use whether by two persons or forty.

The upstairs bedrooms are decorated in individual color schemes and fabrics, giving each a unique feel. With clipped ceilings and individual fireplaces, these upstairs bedrooms have a charm that makes for a memorable visit.

Kitchen

Master bedroom

Master sitting area

Blue bedroom

Yellow bedroom

Red bedroom

Guest bathroom

Green bedroom

Rear elevation with pavilion

WOODLAND HILLS MANOR

Craft House, Atlanta, Georgia, 2006–2008
Mark D. Stevens Builder

Set high on a hill with commanding views overlooking a thick forest of trees, Woodland Hills evokes memories of estates from the grandest traditions. The home is constructed from Wissahickon Schist, a special stone imported from Pennsylvania, and is accented further with Indiana limestone and traditional English roof tiles. Some of the windows are filled with leaded sashes using hand-blown bottle glass, while

Dining room bay window

Limestone front entry

the larger arched windows are steel frame with German Restoration Glass. The impressive limestone front door surround protects the heavy oak door and its leaded glass panels and hand-carved linen-fold panels.

The entry hall is paneled in thick quarter-sawn oak wainscoting, its deeply recessed panels trimmed in wood roping, while the hall's Elizabethan-inspired ceiling is made from wood, painted to resemble plaster. The centerpiece for this hall is the magnificent oak staircase with its 2-inch-thick panels in period style. Each panel was designed and drawn in full scale to accurately adjust for the different length and run of the staircase as it rises.

Dormer, Porch with Gothic arches

Garage bay window

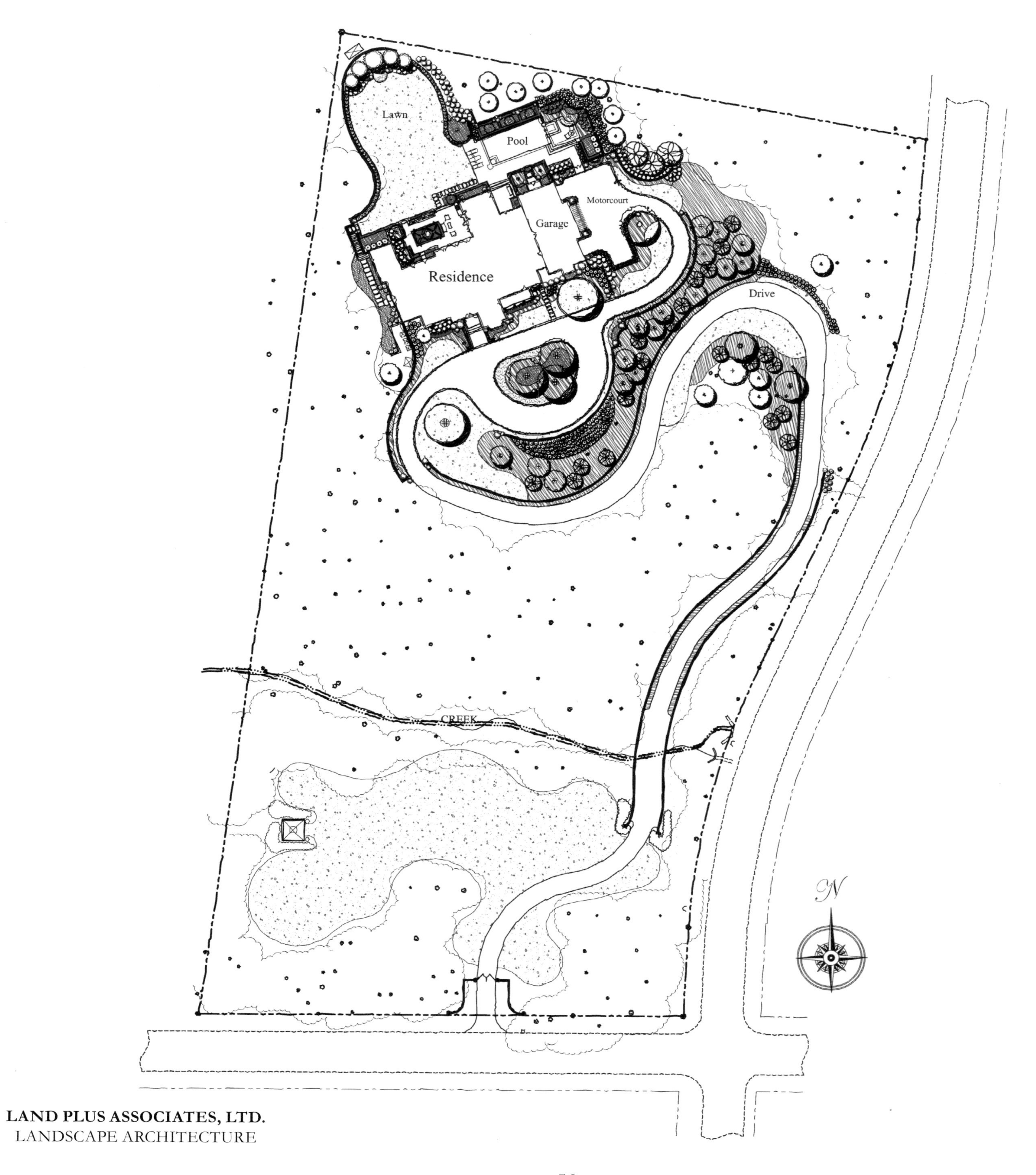

LAND PLUS ASSOCIATES, LTD.
LANDSCAPE ARCHITECTURE

Garage with Arbor

On one side of the foyer is an English pine-paneled study with an elaborate plaster Tudor rose ceiling. The limestone mantle repeats the pointed arch motif found throughout the paneling of the room.

On the other side of the foyer is the dining room which has a lofty cathedral ceiling banded by heavy timbering. At one end of the room, accessed by a hidden door from the second floor, is a minstrel gallery that provides a place for musicians to play during dinner.

The house is designed for comfortable outdoor living as well. The vaulted family room provides a comfortable family sitting area adjoining the kitchen and breakfast room. Its antique wooden beams add warmth and texture to the space. Immediately outside this family room is a covered open air porch

Foyer

Oak staircase

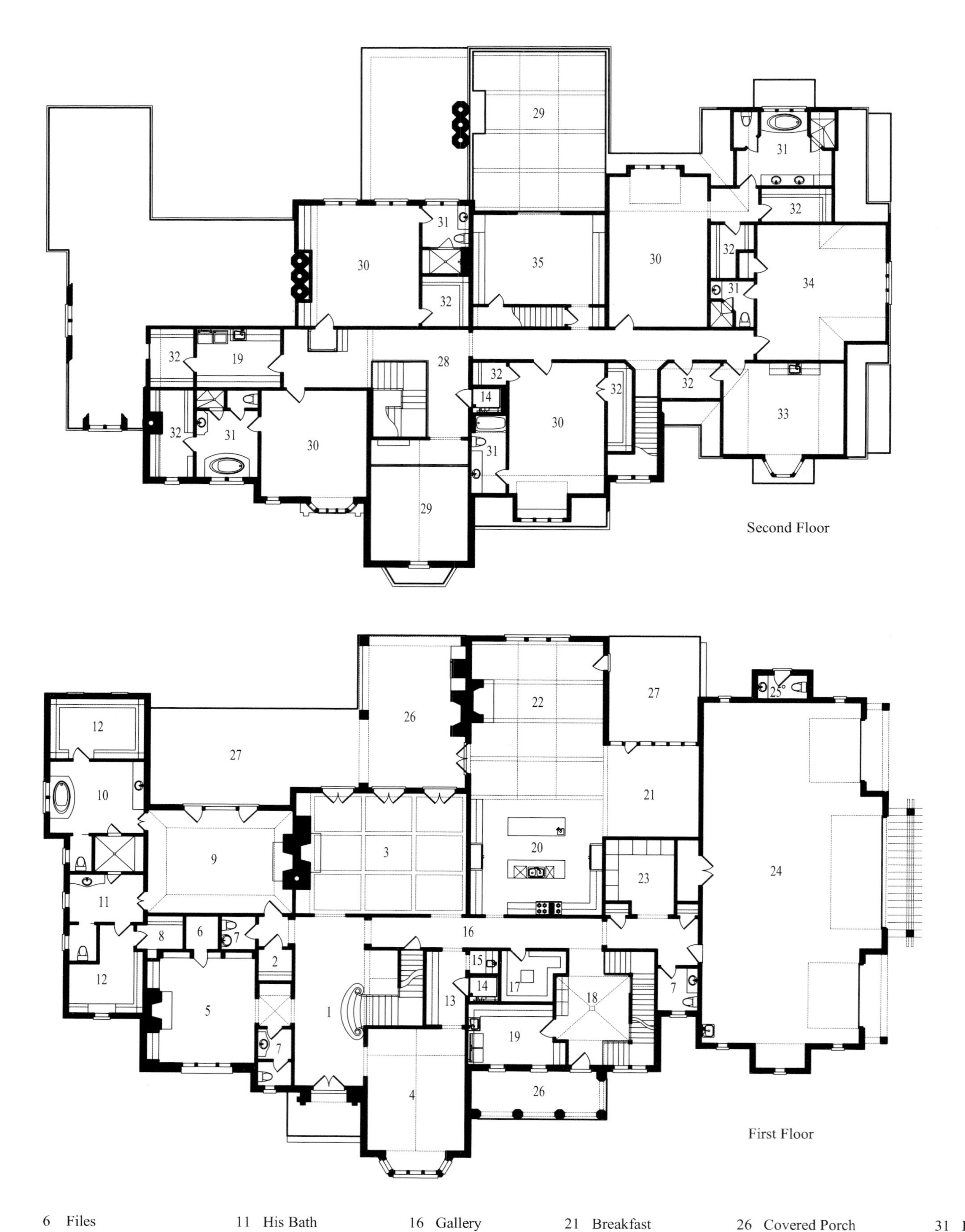

1 Foyer
2 Closet
3 Living Room
4 Dining Room
5 Library
6 Files
7 Powder Room
8 Luggage Closet
9 Master Bedroom
10 Her Bath
11 His Bath
12 Master Closet
13 Butler's Pantry
14 Elevator
15 Wet Bar
16 Gallery
17 Pantry
18 Service Hall
19 Laundry
20 Kitchen
21 Breakfast
22 Family Room
23 Lockers
24 Garage
25 Pool Bath
26 Covered Porch
27 Open Terrace
28 Upper Stair Hall
29 Open to Below
30 Bedroom
31 Bath
32 Closet
33 Art Studio
34 Children's Playroom
35 Study Loft

Foyer paneling detail

Arched opening to study

fitted with a fireplace and barbecue grill for more casual entertaining.

Off the master bedroom is a small enclosed flower garden providing summer color that can be enjoyed from both the porch and the expansive rear lawn. A bluestone terrace and pool surrounded by lush landscaping completes this area, where privacy and elegance abound. The landscape embraces subtle blends of textures and colors to complement the rich hues and materials of the home.

Paneled study

Dining room

Living room

Kitchen

Breakfast room

Family room

Garden off the master bedroom

Brick chimney detail

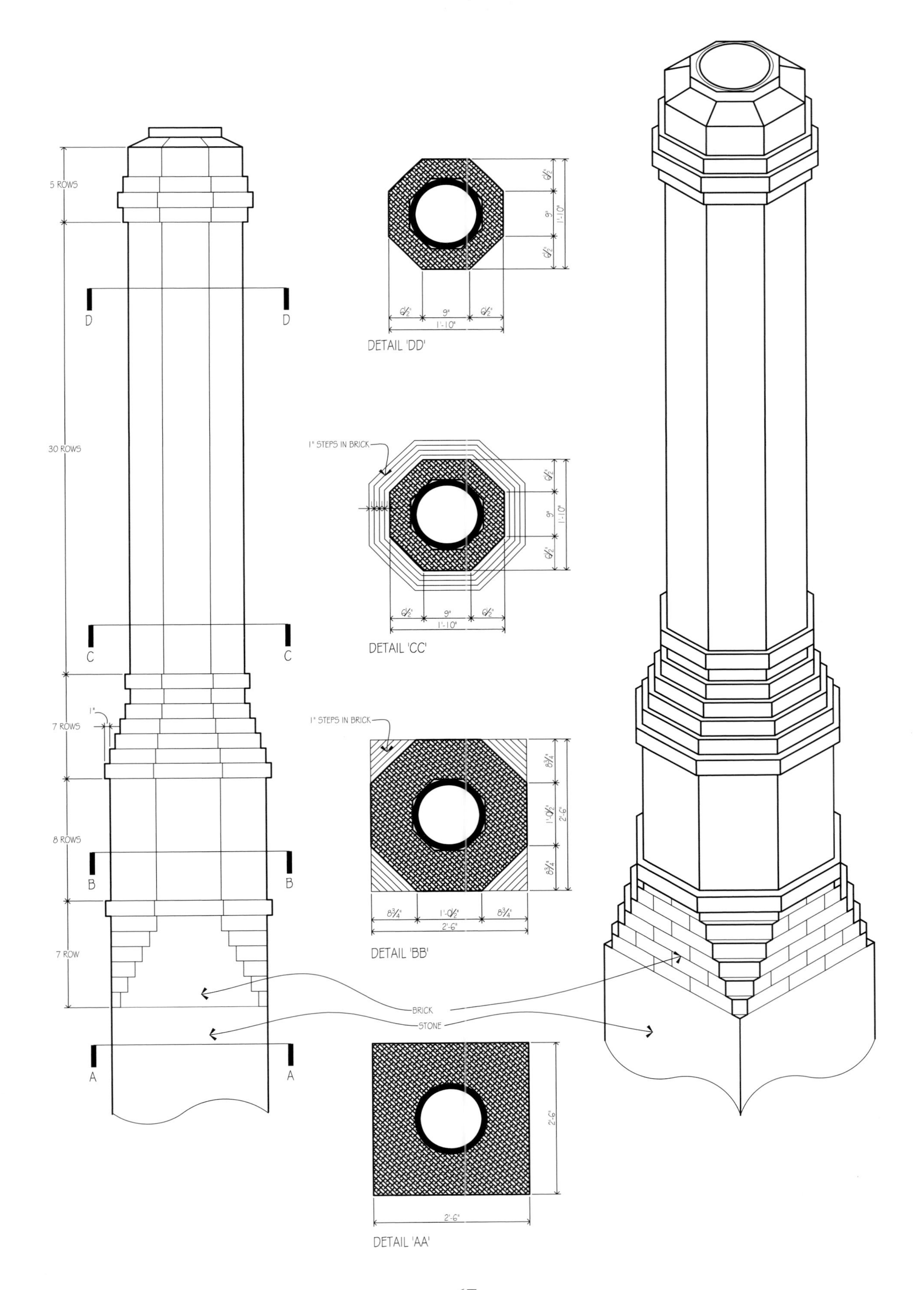

5 ROWS
30 ROWS
7 ROWS
8 ROWS
7 ROW
D
C
B
A
1"
DETAIL 'DD'
DETAIL 'CC'
DETAIL 'BB'
DETAIL 'AA'
1" STEPS IN BRICK
BRICK
STONE
6½"
9"
1'-10"
8¾"
1'-0½"
2'-6"

Garden bench seat

Rear porch

Pool terrace

Detail of front entry

SOUTH OF FRANCE

Tripodi House, Atlanta, Georgia, 2006–2008

Benecki Fine Homes Builder

Interiors by Louis D. Hurr, Santa Barbara, California

Ideally, houses reflect the personality and taste of the owners. The Tripodi house is an accurate representation of the owner's love of all things French. Among the characteristic French provincial design elements found on the exterior of the house is the distinctive tile roof. Each barrel tile is set in a concrete bed and purposefully laid in a not-so-regular manner, creating the effect of great age and charm. Just below the roof, these same tiles have been used at the top of the stucco wall as decorative elements. The windows and doors are painted a soft French blue, as are the horizontal board shutters. The front door is enhanced by a limestone surround with iron railing. The whole effect of the façade is set off by a forecourt of loose gravel set within a cobblestone border. A parterre garden of boxwoods and roses completes the entrance to the house.

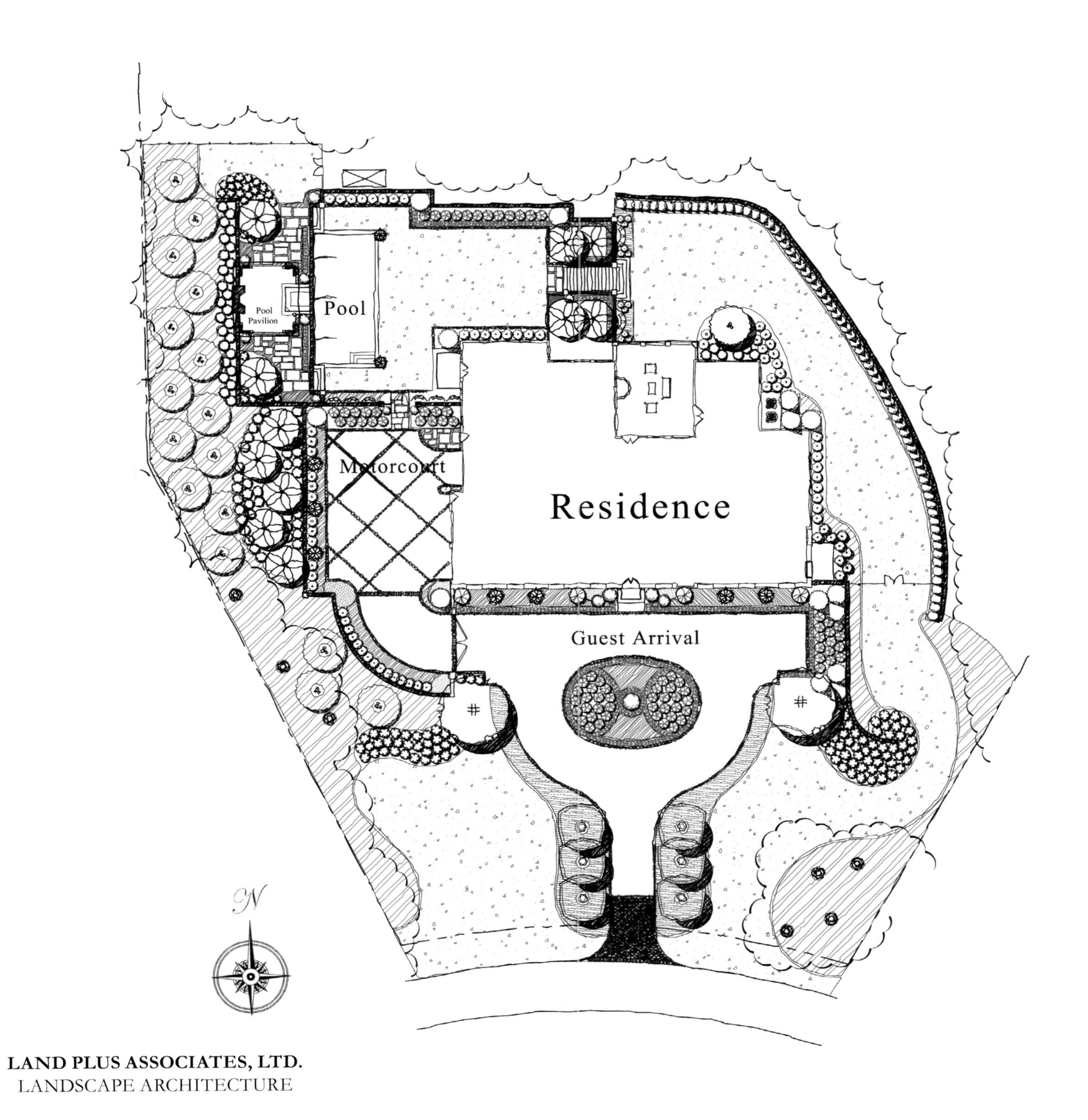

LAND PLUS ASSOCIATES, LTD.
LANDSCAPE ARCHITECTURE

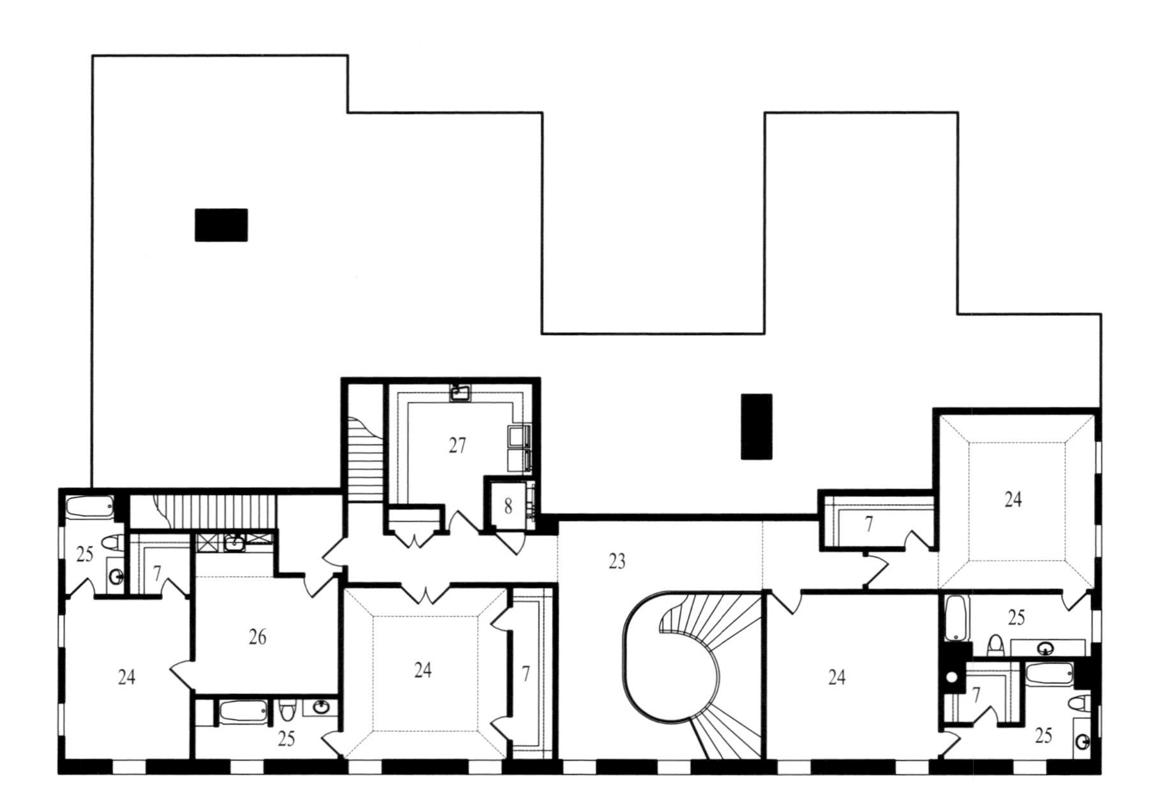

Second Floor

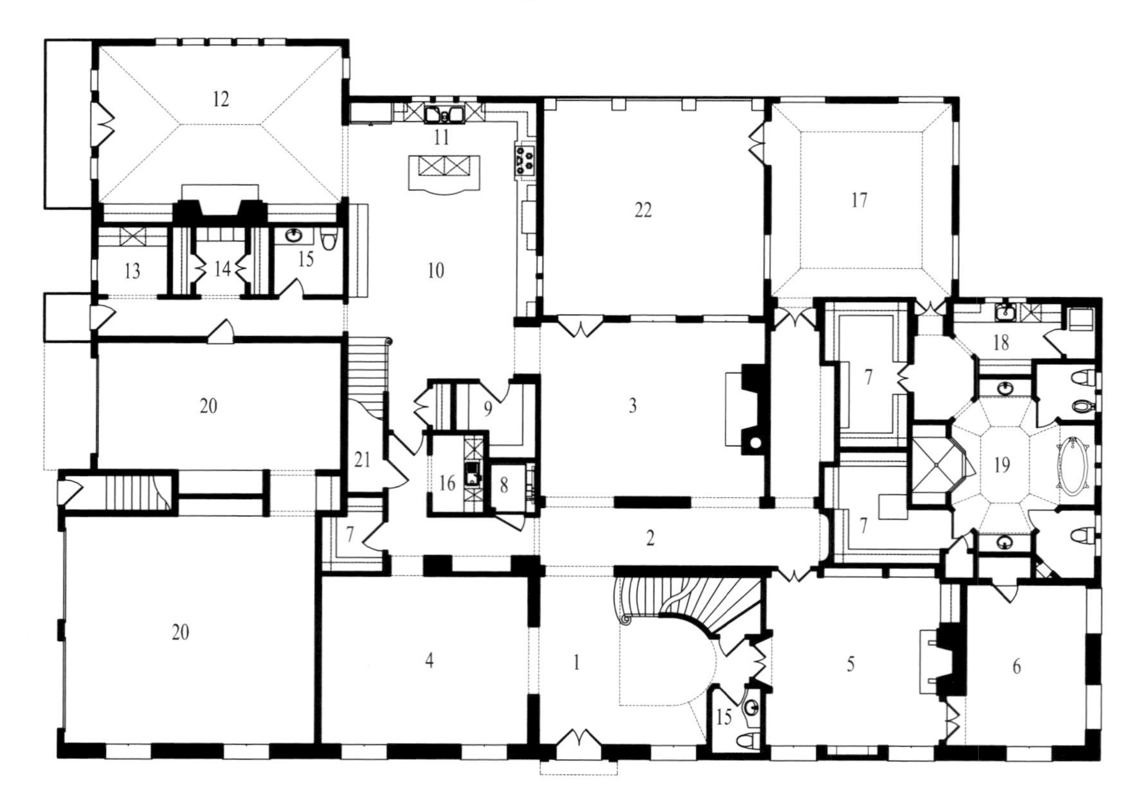

First Floor

1 Foyer
2 Gallery
3 Living Room
4 Dining Room
5 Study
6 Smoking Porch
7 Closet
8 Elevator
9 Pantry
10 Breakfast
11 Kitchen
12 Family Room
13 Office
14 Lockers
15 Mud Bath
16 Butler's Pantry
17 Master Bedroom
18 Morning Kitchen
19 Master Bath
20 Garage
21 Storage
22 Terrace
23 Stair Hall
24 Bedroom
25 Bath
26 Sitting Room
27 Laundry

Foyer staircase

Dining room

The impression of the interiors is one of natural textures and materials. The foyer floor is distressed French limestone and the staircase railing is hand-wrought iron in a simple French pattern. Natural wood timbers accent some of the ceilings. The walls are finished in plaster to complete the feeling of a house in the south of France.

On sunny days, the open air pool pavilion provides welcome shade, while the water spouts projecting from the base of the pavilion create a playful sound in the pool below. During inclement weather, the home's indoor basketball court and home theater are diversions for family and friends. The white plastered wine cellar with its heavy wood table and stocked shelves invites one to linger and enjoy this special house just a little longer.

Living room

Hallway

Porch

THE DOG
NEW CLASSICISTS
IMPRESSIONISM AND
POST-IMPRESSIONISM

Study

Detail of study door

Kitchen

Family room

Master bedroom

Master bathroom

Indoor basketball court

Wine cellar

Pool cabana

Front elevation

A Family's Mountain Retreat

Beskin Cottage, Cashiers, North Carolina, 2006–2008

Dearl Stewart Builder

Interiors by Kathleen Rivers, Charleston, South Carolina

Many local families have a tradition of escaping the oppressive heat of the Georgia summer by retreating to the mountains of North Carolina during the hottest months. The Beskin family enjoys this tradition and constructed their stone and shake-shingle mountain house as a family retreat for golf, hiking, and entertaining during these months. The house's high elevation provides cool breezes and wide vistas of distant rocky peaks.

The skin of the house is composed of large sheets of tree bark that have been steamed into flat sheets. The texture and color of the bark complements the rugged indigenous

Front door detail

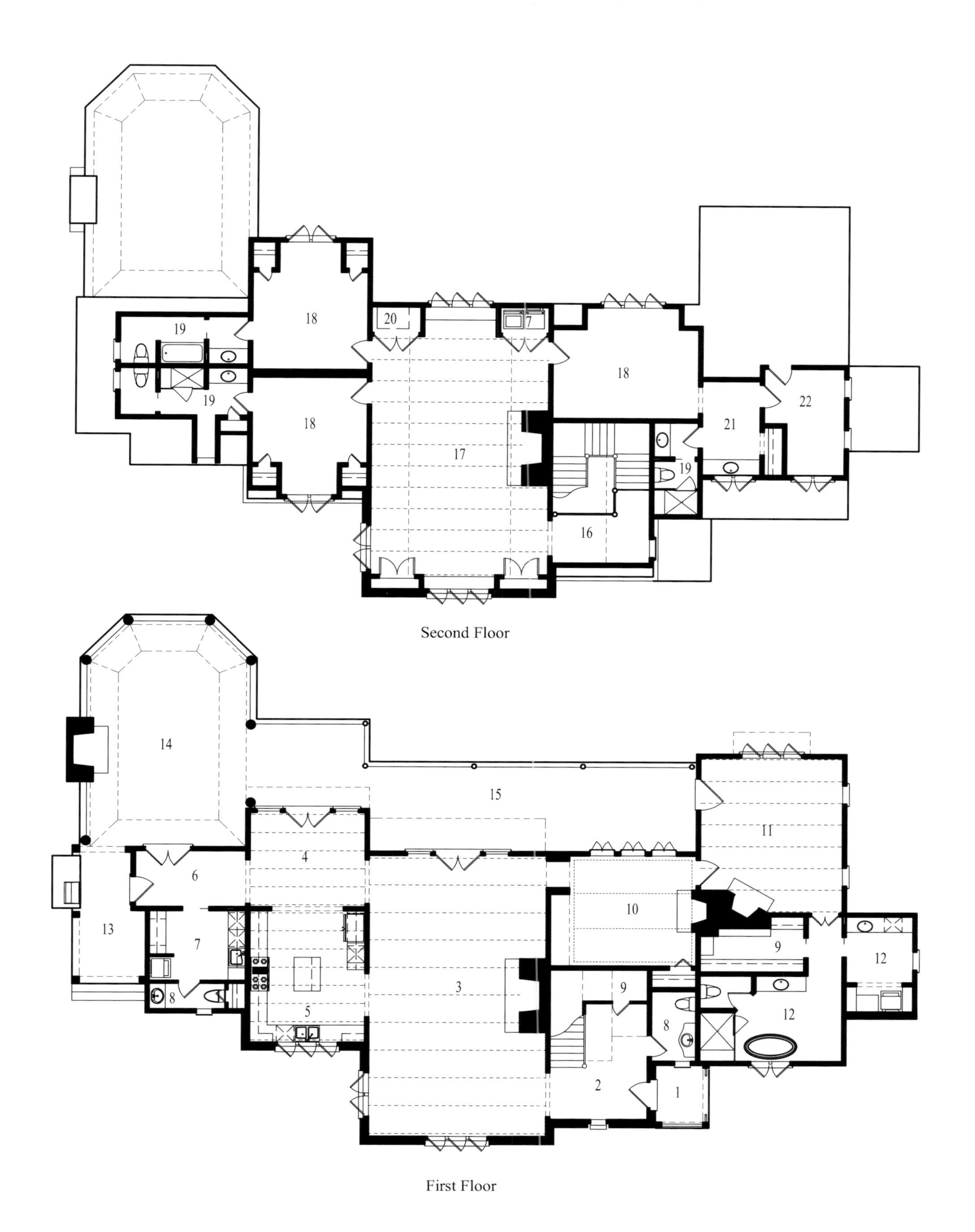

1 Front Porch	5 Kitchen	9 Closet	13 Grill Porch	17 Upstairs Sitting	21 Dressing Room
2 Foyer	6 Service Hall	10 Study	14 Covered Porch	18 Bedroom	22 Nursery
3 Great Room	7 Laundry	11 Master Bedroom	15 Open Deck	19 Bath	
4 Breakfast	8 Powder Room	12 Master Bath	16 Stair Hall	20 Mechanical Room	

Entry hall

Stair hall

Upper stair hall

Dining room

Living room

Kitchen

Breakfast room

mountain rock, adding more texture to the façade. The columns and railings of the porch are made from locust trees. The bark has been preserved to enhance the rustic look, as does the cedar shake roof.

In an effort to create an all-wood look for the interior, reclaimed wood planks and massive hand-hewn beams from old barns were used extensively on the walls and ceilings. Even the staircase railing makes

Master sitting room

use of log timbers. The home's many fireplaces are lined with granite instead of firebrick and have monolithic slabs of stone above the firebox openings. All the floors are made of wide-plank heart-of-pine, with cracks and imperfections carefully preserved for their charm.

No trip to the mountains would be complete without the family's dogs. So, in the pantry, concealed under a counter

Master bedr

of rough-cut wood, the home incorporates a specially designated area for the dogs' beds.

Stepping out of the house to the rear deck and porch,

Rear hall

Dog bed alcove

one is immediately struck by the beauty of the mountain views. The covered porch is built from locust logs and is the focus of evening dinners by the stone fireplace. Hewn

Side entrance porch

limbs are woven into a decorative lattice detail that runs from top of column to top of column. Sitting on the porch at night, one can hear the sound of tree frogs calling their mates while the hoots and calls of owls fill the air.

Rear porch with stone fireplace

GLEN DEVON HOUSE

Atlanta, Georgia, 2006–2008
Benecki Fine Homes Builder
Interiors and interior architecture by James Michael Howard, Atlanta, Georgia

Granite cobblestones line the driveway leading to this French-inspired home. Its two projecting wings on the front façade enclose a bluestone walkway that leads to the front entry. A minimalist iron-and-glass canopy above the door supports a gas lantern hanging above the entry. On each side of the entry walk, the landscaping echoes the minimalist look of the architecture with its carpet of dwarf Mondo grass laid between the two boxwood parterre gardens.

Stepping through a pair of walnut doors, one enters an expansive foyer that connects the principal rooms with a gallery hall leading to the study and master suite. The dark wide-plank hardwood floors provide

Front door with iron canopy

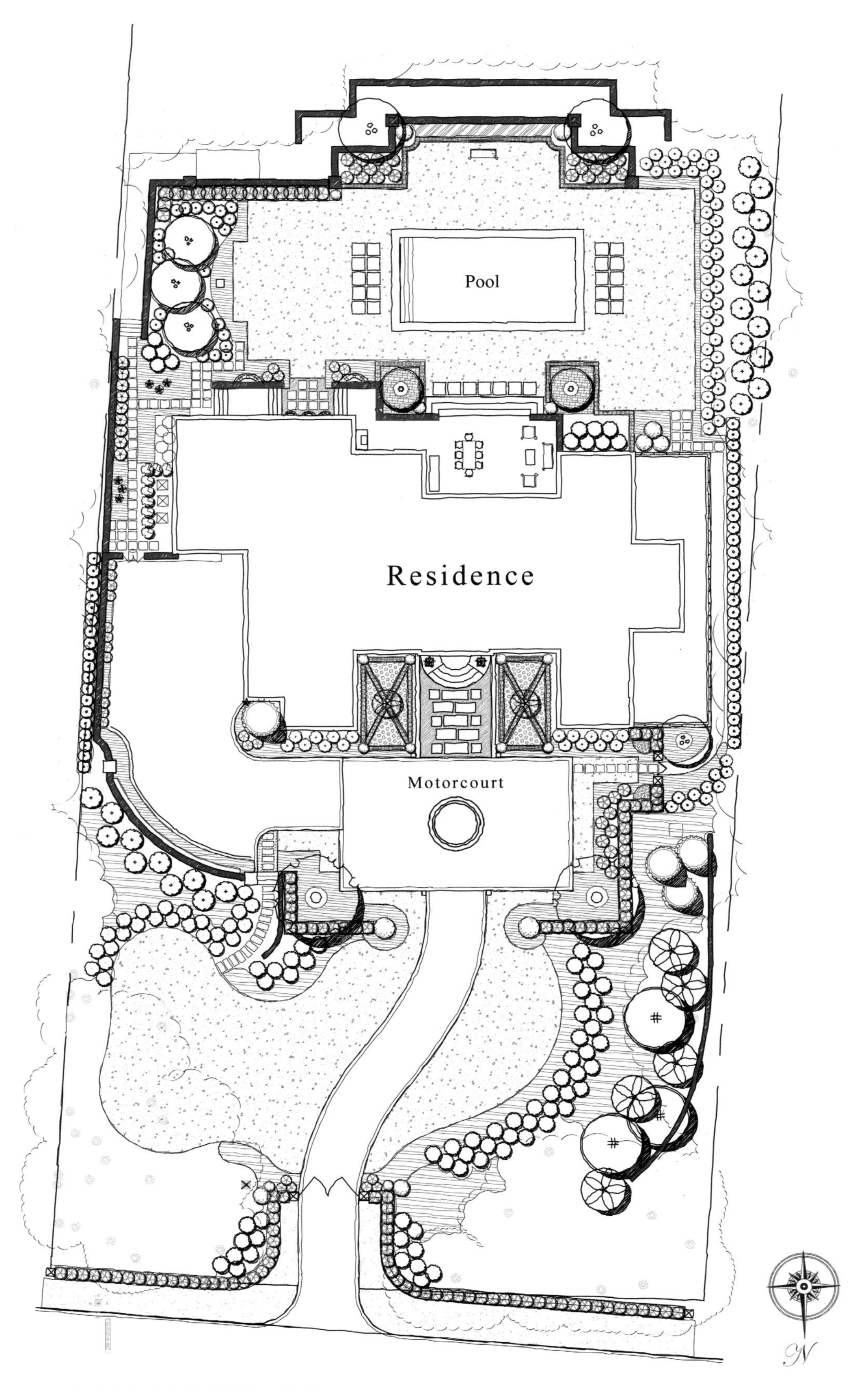

LAND PLUS ASSOCIATES, LTD.
LANDSCAPE ARCHITECTURE

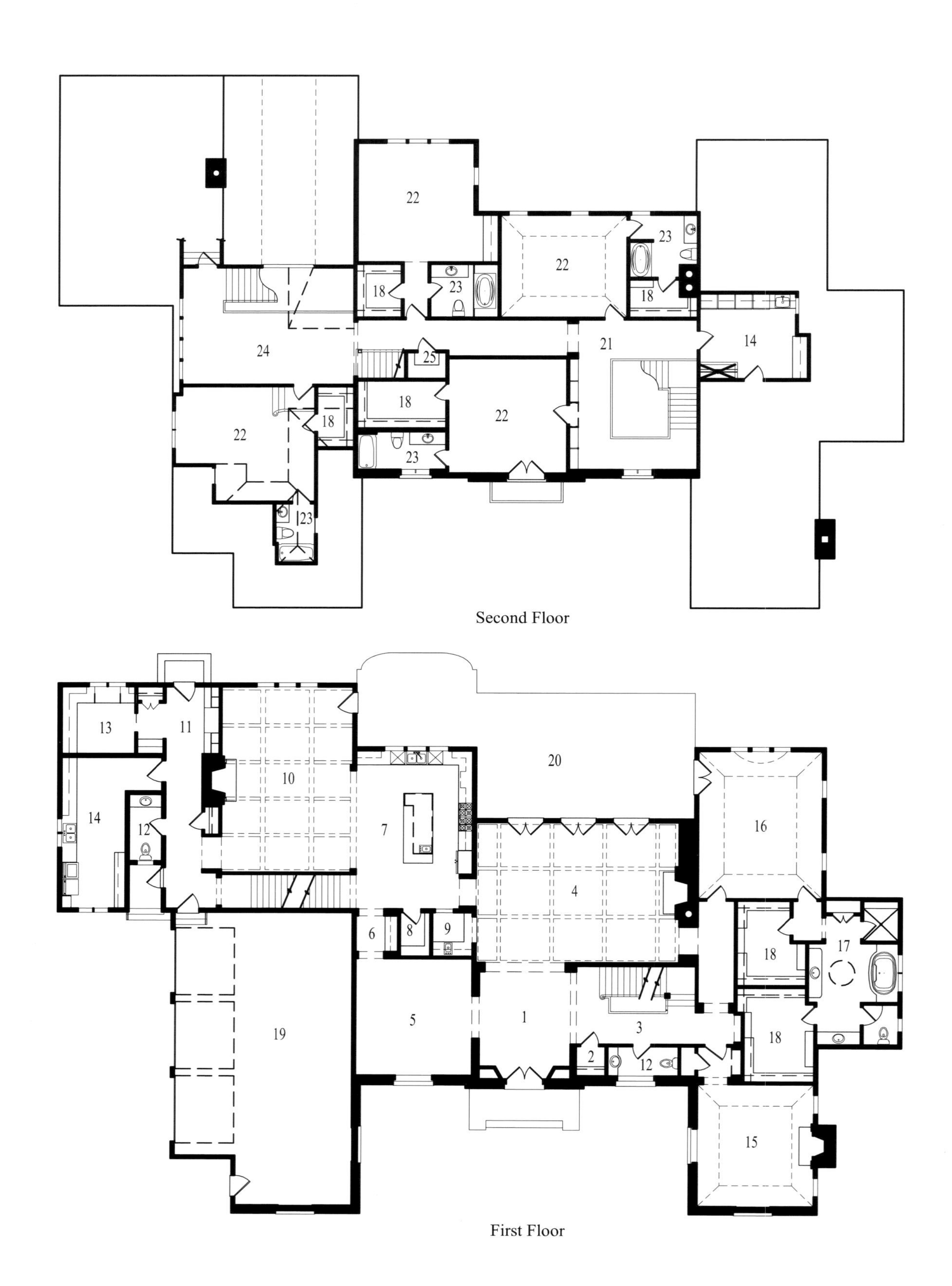

1 Foyer
2 Closet
3 Stair Hall
4 Living Room
5 Dining Room
6 Butler's Pantry
7 Kitchen
8 Pantry
9 Wet Bar
10 Family Room
11 Service Hall
12 Half Bath
13 Office
14 Laundry
15 Study
16 Master Bedroom
17 Master Bath
18 Closet
19 Garage
20 Terrace
21 Upper Stair Hall
22 Bedroom
23 Bath
24 Children's Study
25 Linen

Stair hall

Living room

Living room fireplace

a deep contrast to the soft hues of the sophisticated interiors. The dining room walls are paneled in a simple wood pattern painted a soft grey; an iron-and-wood chandelier completes the look. On an axis with the main entry is the living room. With no moldings and a coved ceiling, the architecture of this room dissolves away, highlighting the furnishings and the room's limestone mantle. The kitchen opens directly to the

Study

Dining room

Kitchen

Family room

Her closet

Master bedroom

Guest bedroom

family room with its vaulted ceiling and large window that echoes the same design in the master suite.

The master wing is designed to provide a quiet retreat and looks out to the pool beyond. The dramatic vaulted ceiling in the bedroom is wrapped in painted beams, framing the large window that floods the room with

Guest bedroom

sunlight during the day. Down the adjoining hallway, a pine-paneled study provides a private space for reading or working late at night.

Framed within an elegant lawn panel, and surrounded by lush landscaping, the pool and stone terrace provide an inviting area that is ideal for those nights when the cool evening air makes entertaining outdoors a delight.

Lower level game room

Lower level kitchen

Terrace with seating

Terrace with outdoor dining

Rear elevation

MEMORIES OF ENGLAND

Thurlow, Atlanta, Georgia, 2006–2008
Ron Lester, Builder
Interiors by Rabaut Design Associates, Atlanta, Georgia

Building a new home that blends successfully with the established fabric of a historic neighborhood requires special sensitivity to style and scale. Because the house is located in the city's historic Garden Hills district, the Kendall family chose to build a home in keeping with the English-style homes that were popular in the neighborhood during the 1920s.

The house was carefully designed to hide its three-car garage, a feat of no small consequence, given the narrow urban lot. With its successful attention to proportion and detail, the finished home is a welcome addition to the street.

Owner's initials above front entry

Detail of front-door surround

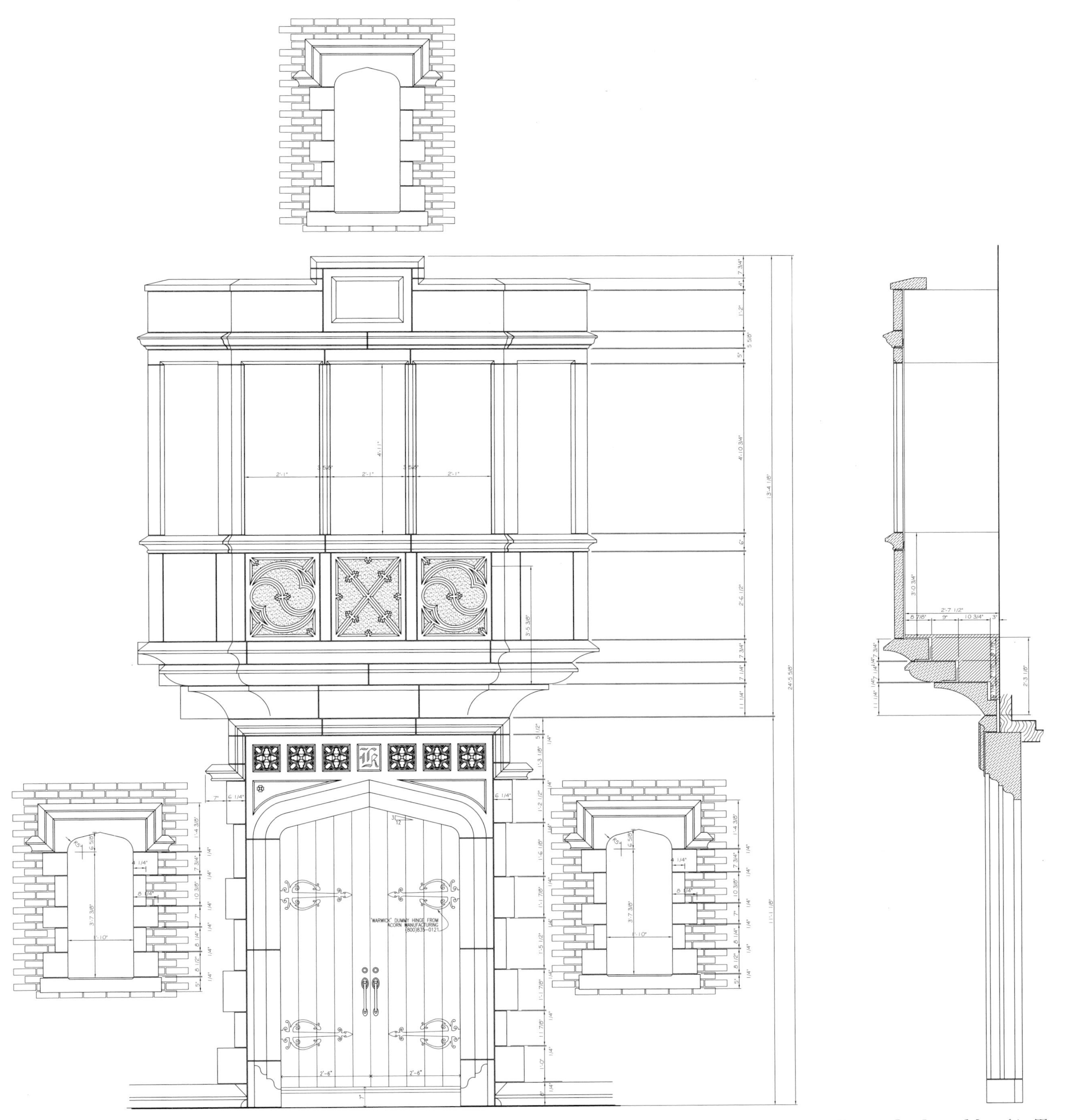

Christie Cut Stone, Memphis, Tennessee

Foyer window alcove

The home's craftsmanship is a testament to the skill of the building team. A spectacular hand-carved limestone bay window, cantilevered from the face of the house, is an

Living room

engineering feat and represents the acumen of the builder. Flemish-bond brickwork and a heavy slate roof are authentic to the period, as are the diamond-paned, leaded glass windows, which reflect the evening light in a myriad of patterns. Bound by hand-wrought iron-strap hinges, the heavy, timbered front doors take inspiration from a 16th-century English manor house. At the back of the house, a covered rear porch, pool with a flagstone terrace, pool house, children's play area, and koi pond provide areas for outdoor dining and recreation.

Dining room

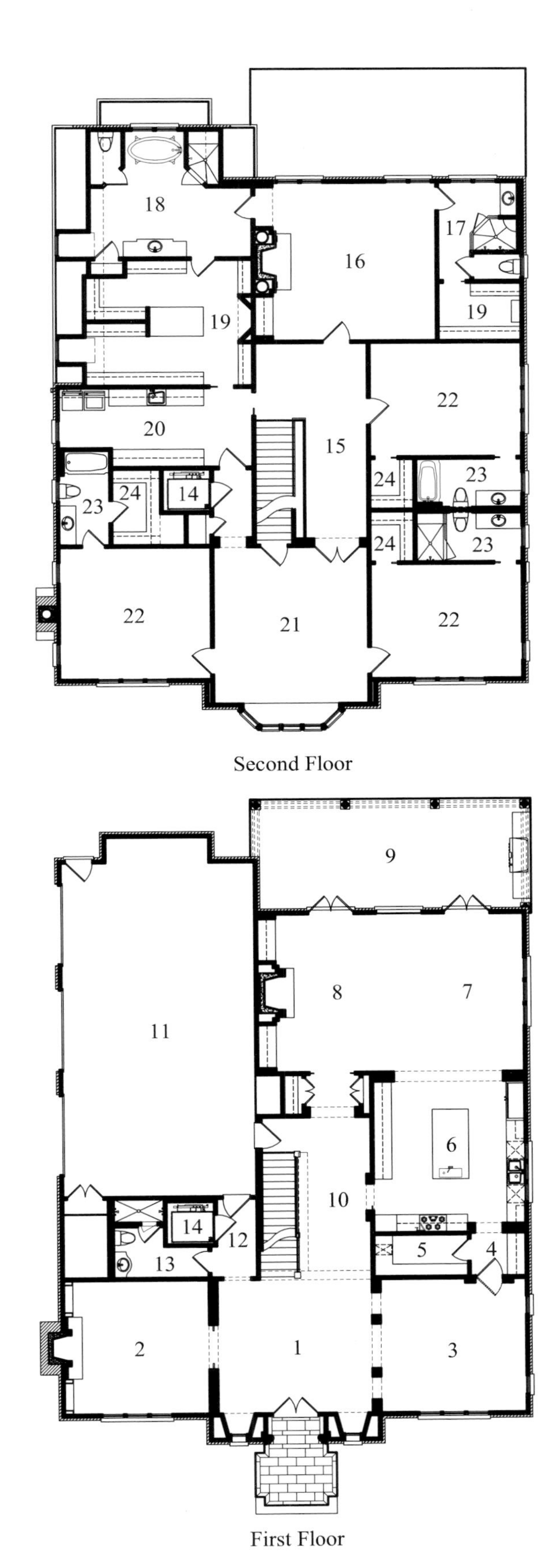

Second Floor

First Floor

1 Foyer
2 Living Room
3 Dining Room
4 Butler's Pantry
5 Pantry
6 Kitchen
7 Breakfast Area
8 Family Sitting
9 Loggia
10 Stair Hall
11 Garage
12 Garage Entry
13 Hall Bath
14 Elevator
15 Upper Stair Hall
16 Master Bedroom
17 His Bath
18 Her Bath
19 Master Closet
20 Laundry
21 Sitting Room
22 Bedroom
23 Bath
24 Closet

Family room

Kitchen

Inside the house, Thurlow's interiors successfully incorporate the traditional Tudor Revival-style architecture of the exterior with a lighter, more transitional aesthetic aimed at comfortable family living. A springlike color palette and emphasis on views to the outdoors lend energy and freshness to each room. Designing a historically inspired house that offers the livability of a modern-day house can be challenging. Both inside and out, the Kendall family's home, Thurlow, achieves this balance with style and grace.

Wine cellar

Master bedroom

Master closet

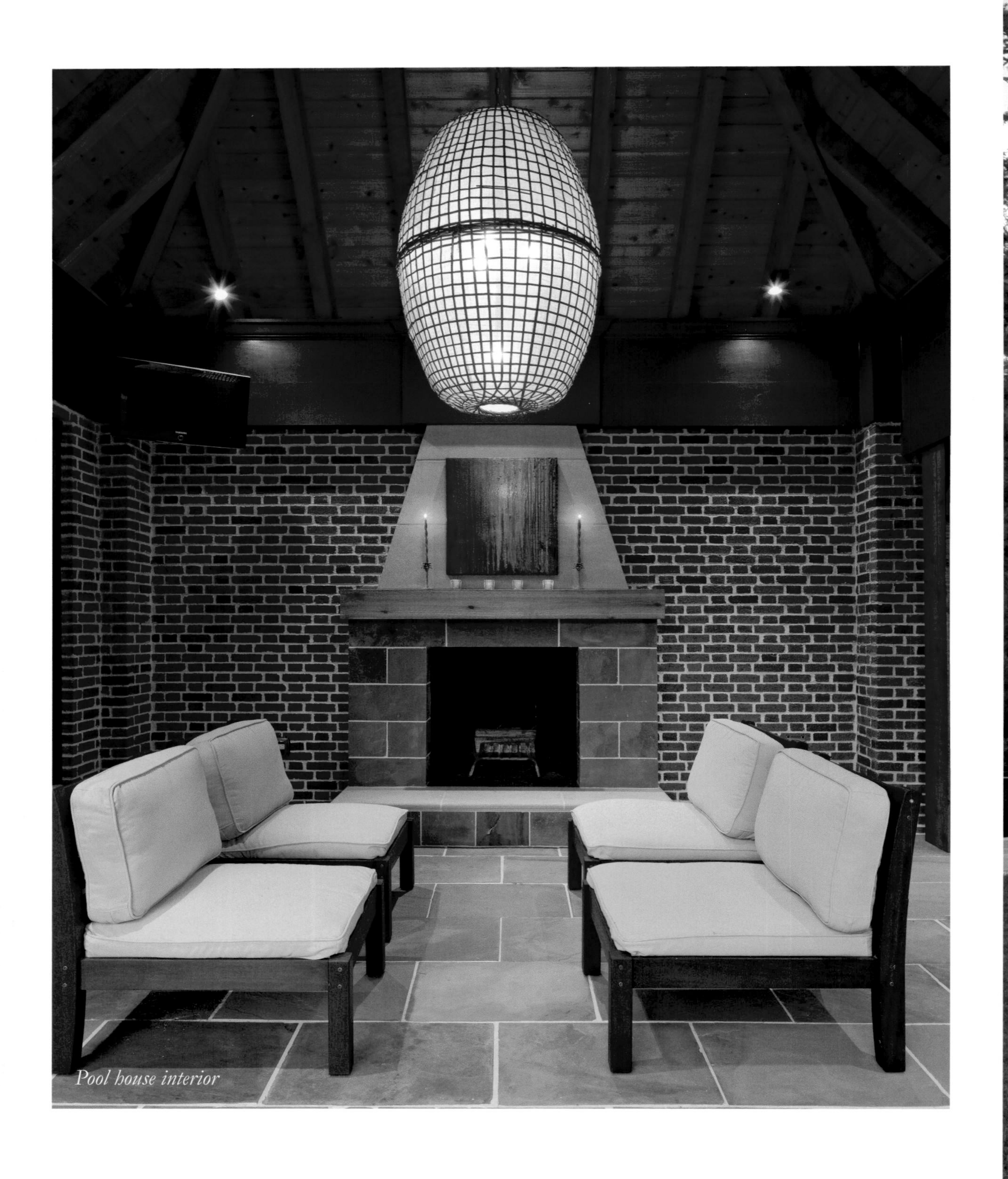
Pool house interior

Rear elevation

A Marsh Home on Sea Island

Smith Cottage, Sea Island, Georgia, 2007–2008

Frank Serafini Builder

Original Architect Ed Cheshire, St. Simons Island, Georgia

Interiors by the Owner and Gerry Burge of Allenbrooke Interiors, Alpharetta, Georgia

Sea Island, Georgia has long been a popular choice for families wanting a second home at a beach and golf resort. Located on the Atlantic coast, Sea Island was developed in the late 1920s and soon became a luxury golf resort destination patronized by such golfing legends as Bobby Jones and Charles Yates. The center of the island's social life is the Cloister, a Mediterranean-style hotel originally designed by

Sunset over the salt marsh

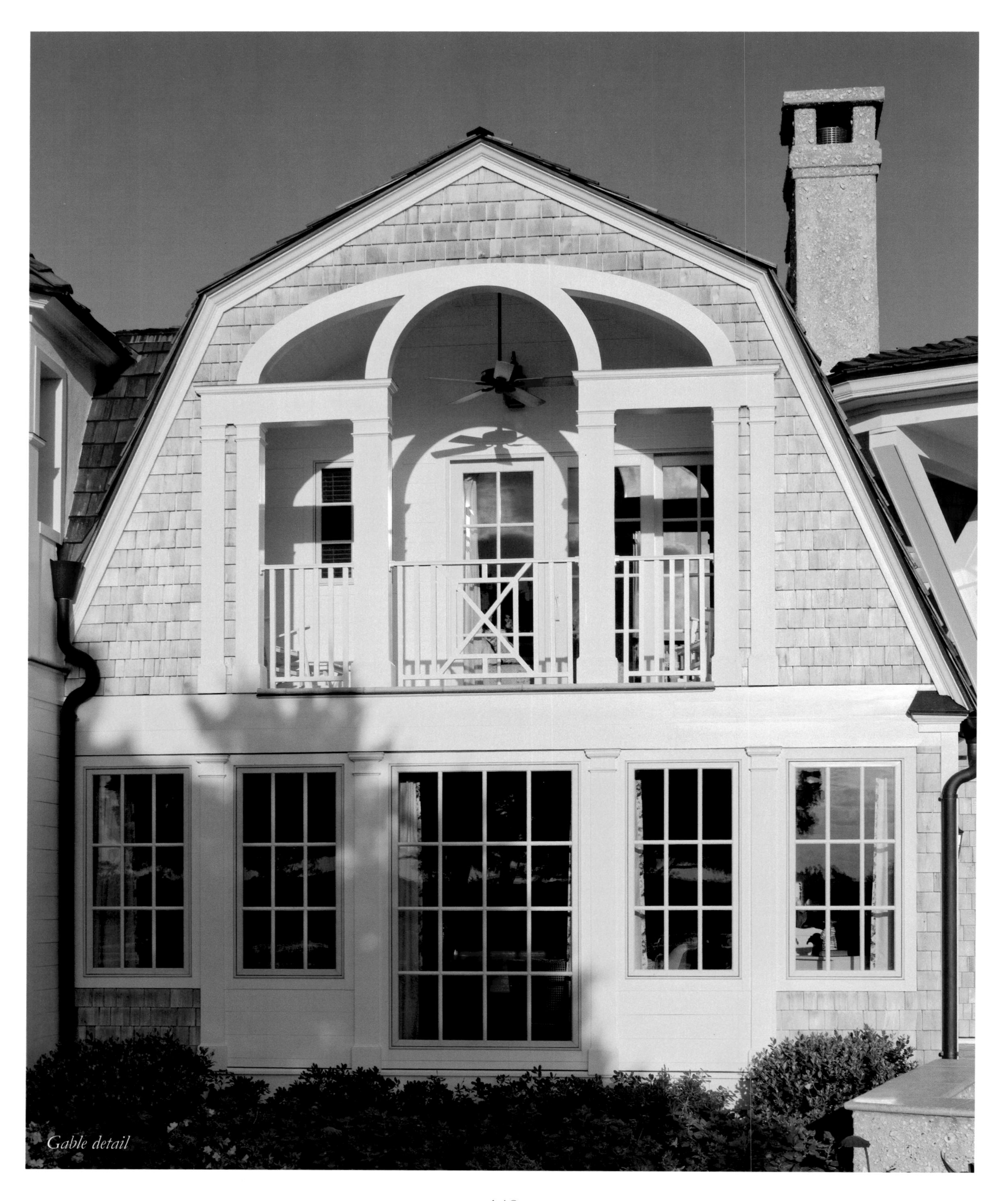

Gable detail

Garage dormer detail

Garage door detail

Living room detail

Addison Mizner in the grand tradition of Palm Beach and Boca Raton. The Cloister is well known for its mix of casual family friendliness and sophisticated club life. The cottages that were built on Sea Island during this era were inspired by the Mediterranean resort architecture of the hotel and reflect the

Living room

"Roaring Twenties" love affair with this casual yet elegant architecture.

Sea Island is bordered by the ocean on its east side and surrounded by a tidal saltwater marsh on its west. Many of the island's cottages have a view of either the Atlantic Ocean or of the "ocean" of gold-colored sea grass across the western salt marsh.

Dining room

Kitchen and Family room

The Smith family has roots in New England and was attracted to the Shingle Style made famous by architects such as McKim, Mead, and White in the late 1800s and early 1900s. They admired the expansive view across the salt marsh and hired Baker to embark on a

Kitchen cooktop

Master bedroom

total rebuilding of the interiors and a major expansion and enhancement of the house's architecture. The family's primary residence is also a William T. Baker design.

The cottage was originally constructed in 1987 and needed remodeling and updating. The Smiths used the opportunity to enlarge the master suite, add a paneled study, and

Paneled study

Art studio

Son's bedroom

enlarge the kitchen, family room, and garage. This also provided Baker the opportunity to enhance the cottage's architecture with new details characteristic of Shingle Style. The new second-floor porches with their large arched openings greatly enhance the rear façade. The view of the marsh from the upstairs porches and bedrooms is especially magnificent at sunset, when the glow of the last rays of light falls across the golden reeds of the marsh. The resulting residence is a dramatic and elegant addition to the architecture of Sea Island.

Rear elevation before remodel

Rear elevation after remodel

A Designer's Own Home

Woodward House, Atlanta, Georgia, 2007–2008
Jon Bernesden Builder
Interiors by Suzanne Kasler, Atlanta, Georgia

Designing a home in collaboration with one of America's foremost interior designers presents a unique opportunity. The home of John Morris and his wife Suzanne Kasler proved to be just that, as it incorporates many of Kasler's concepts and ideas for gracious living into the context of traditional Georgian architecture.

Window detail

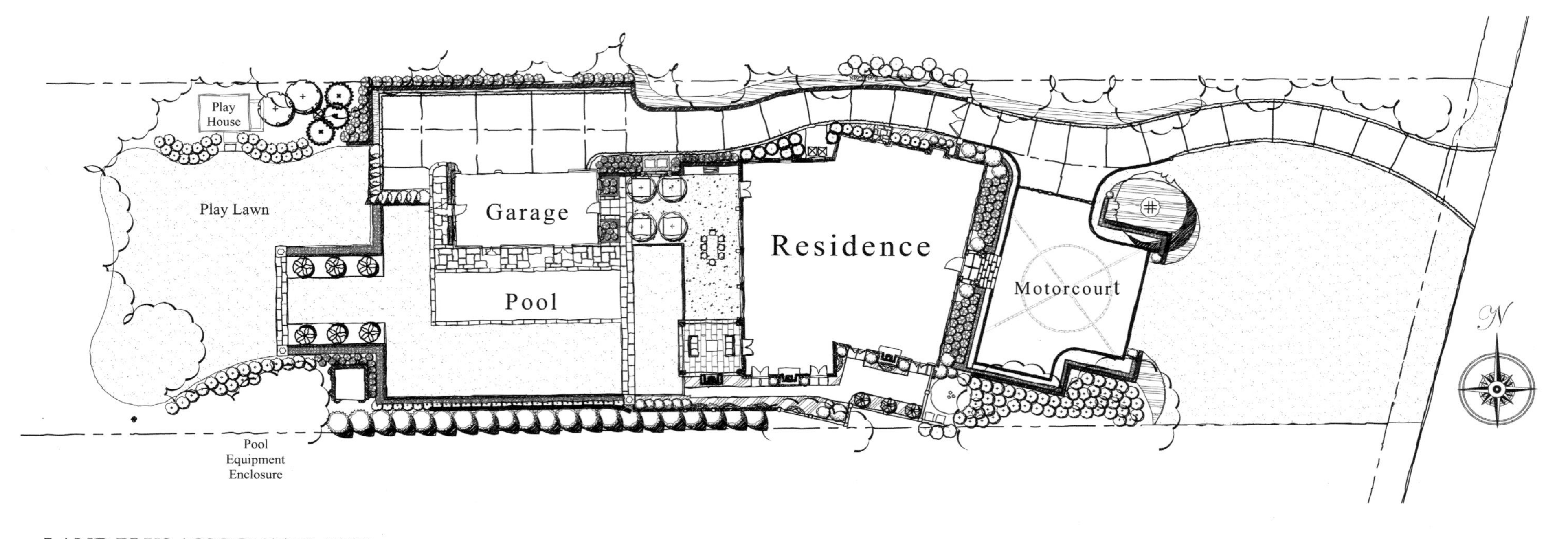

LAND PLUS ASSOCIATES, LTD.
LANDSCAPE ARCHITECTURE

Pool equipment building, drawing by Landplus Associates

Detail of limestone front porch

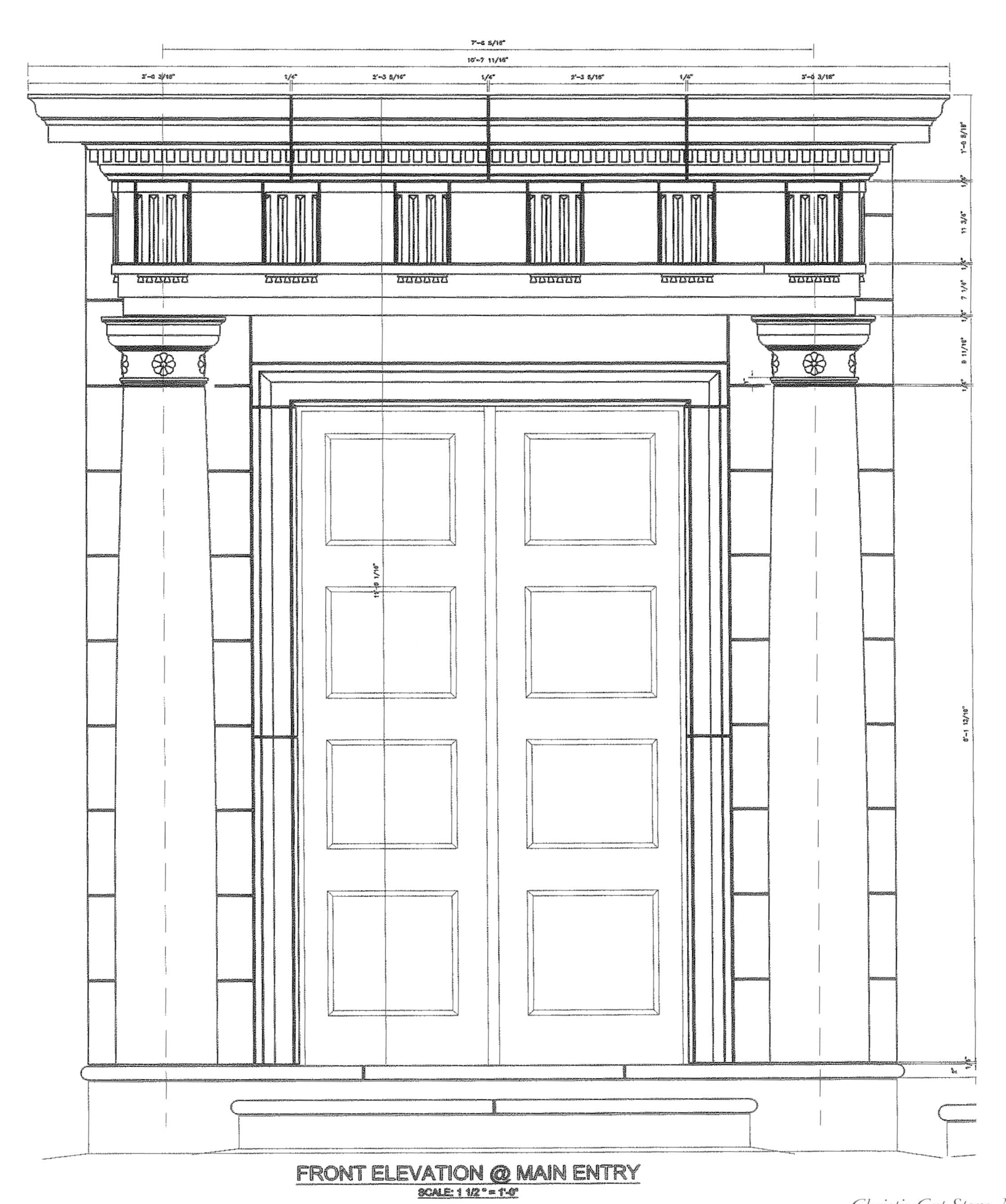

Christie Cut Stone, Memphis, Tennessee

Second Floor

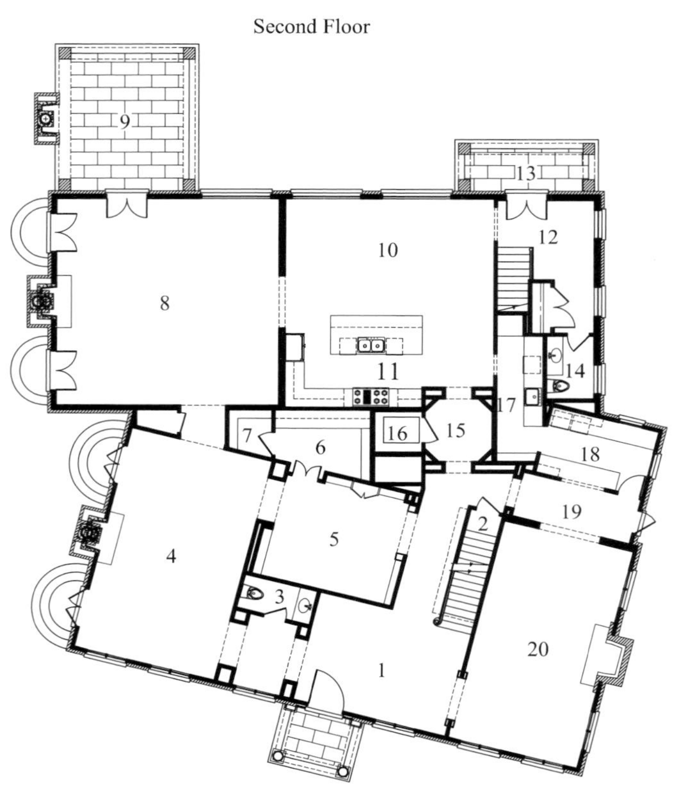

First Floor

1 Foyer
2 Closet
3 Powder Room
4 Living Room
5 Paneled Study
6 Office
7 File Storage
8 Family Room
9 Rear Porch
10 Breakfast Area
11 Kitchen
12 Rear Hall
13 Rear Porch
14 Half Bath
15 Vestibule
16 Elevator
17 Caterer's Kitchen
18 Bar
19 Side Entry Hall
20 Dining Room
21 Stair Hall
22 Hall
23 Bedroom
24 Bathroom
25 Closet
26 Laundry Room
27 Master Sitting Room
28 Master Bedroom
29 Master Closet
30 Master Bathroom

Foyer

The core of the house was an existing house with a center hall plan. The scope of work, however, doubled the size of the existing house and reoriented the back half of the house on axis with the rear lawn and new pool. A three-car detached garage with guest suite above was added. Incorporating these additions in a seamless manner required deft attention to the scale of the roof and continuation of architectural detail.

Living room

The original red-brick exterior was painted a soft white and accented with limestone details such as the simple lintels above the French doors, the stone banding under the second floor windows, and the beautiful limestone porch at the front entry. The variegated grey slate roof provides the perfect contrast to the cool color of the brick and stone. The steel casement windows at the rear of the home provide open views of

Dining room

the gravel terrace and the green lawn extending to the very edge of the pool.

On entering the house, one is greeted by the surprise of a reconfigured entry hall having the stairs off to one side. The diamond-pane detail of the limestone lintels is repeated on the panels of the front door and again on the main staircase. Going from room to room, one notices that the trim of each room is playfully different. The entry hall has a fluted frieze while the dining room has a mirrored frieze overlaid with pierced fretwork. The elegant paneled study has an articulated cornice and a concealed door that opens to a working office.

As a further reflection of Suzanne Kasler's style and taste, the kitchen has a minimalist effect in contrast to the formal entertainment rooms. The plaster-finish hood above the gas cooker top is restrained in its simplicity, as is the cabinetry. The family room adjoining the kitchen is a soothing retreat and opens to the covered porch and its outdoor fireplace. This external room is the perfect setting for casual daily living.

Paneled study

Kitchen

Kitchen eating area

Family room

Rear service staircase

Doorway to master suite

Master sitting room

Master bedroom

Master bathroom tub area

Dressing area in Master bathroom

Pool and rear lawn

Pool house and garage

Rear porch and fireplace

HUDSON HOUSE

Hudson House, Columbus, Georgia 2004–2007
Ben Parham Builder

Building a family home is a labor of love. In this case, after years spent looking for the ideal property, the family's patience was rewarded when they acquired this large property with lake views from the rear terrace. This expansive property with its broad lawn lends itself to a Georgian-style house. Georgian-style homes are characterised by symmetrical and balanced façades. However, achieving a symmetrical façade is often difficult, with the needs of today's lifestyles and multiple-car garages. Yet with deep offsets to the floor plan and careful landscaping, the house achieves this perfection of balance and symmetry.

The core of the house is designed around a graceful curved staircase that embraces the two-story space. The balcony completes the curve and gives scale to the open space below. Finely detailed arches open to the principal entertainment

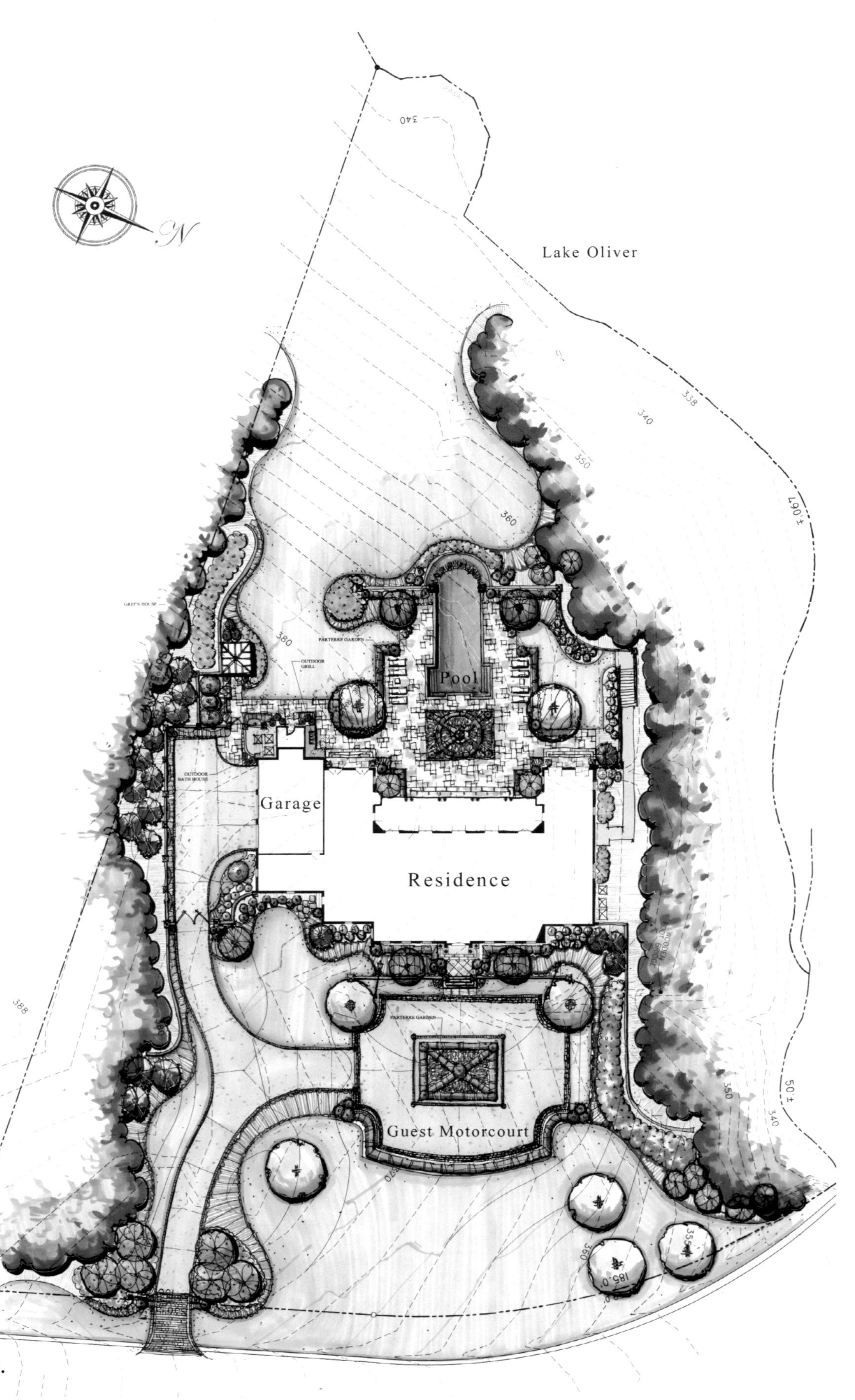

LAND PLUS ASSOCIATES, LTD.
LANDSCAPE ARCHITECTURE

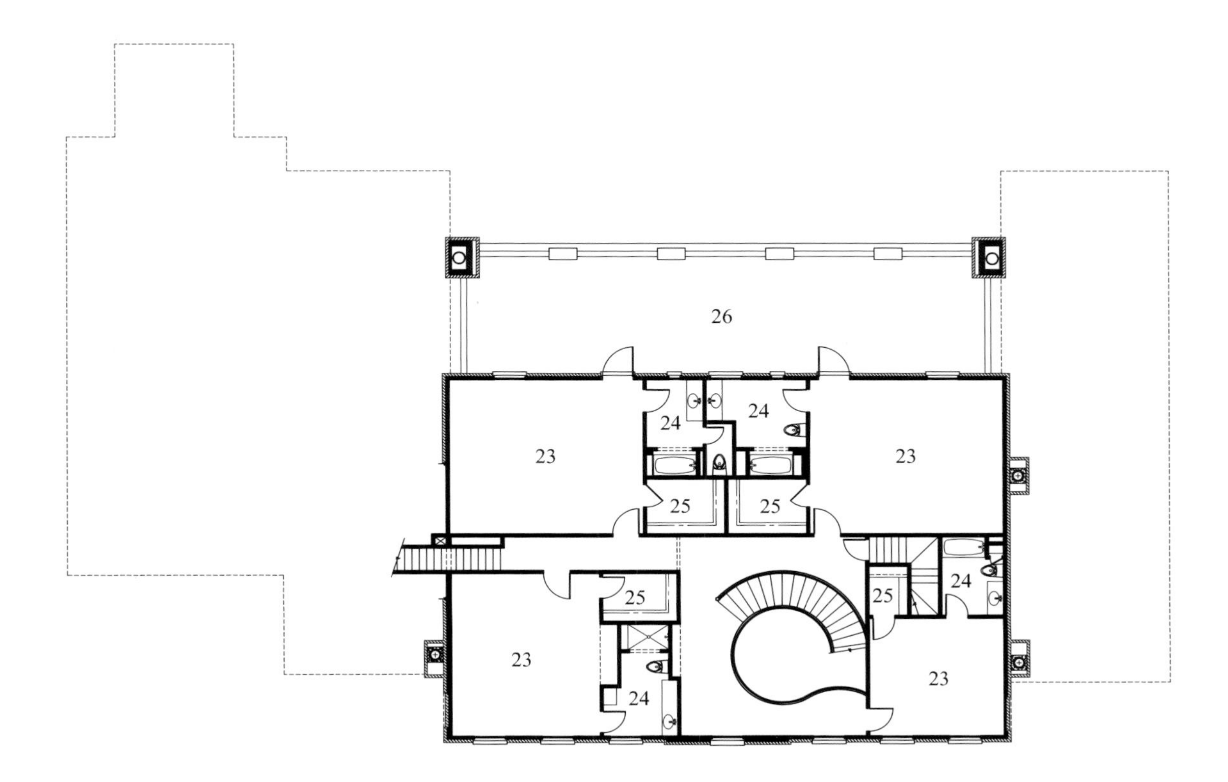

Second Floor

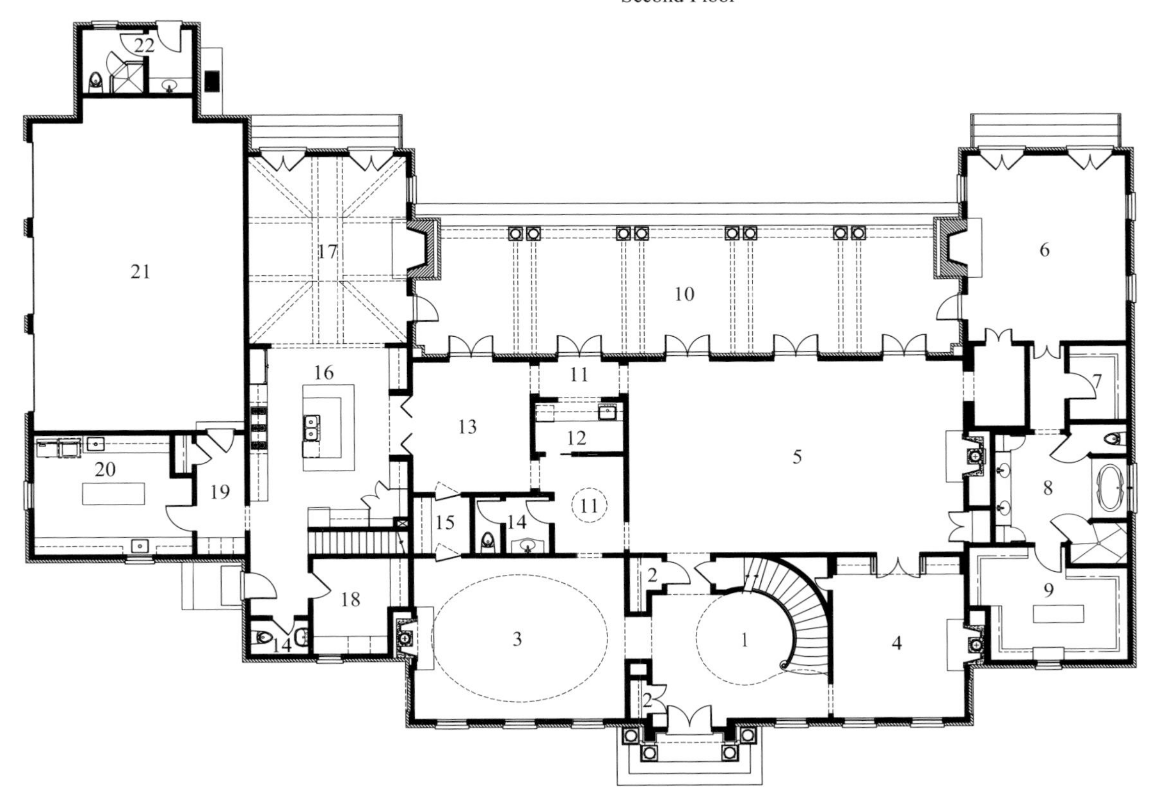

First Floor

1 Foyer
2 Closet
3 Dining Room
4 Paneled Study
5 Living Room
6 Master Bedroom
7 His Closet
8 Master Bathroom
9 Her Closet
10 Loggia
11 Hall
12 Bar
13 Breakfast Room
14 Powder Room
15 Butler's Pantry
16 Kitchen
17 Vaulted Family Room
18 Office
19 Garage Entry
20 Laundry Room
21 Garage
22 Pool Bath
23 Bedroom
24 Bathroom
25 Closet
26 Open Terrace

Foyer

Molding detail with chair

Door detail

rooms. The focal point for the large dining room is a painting by English-born American artist Thomas Sully (1783–1872) that hangs above the mantle. The study, with its painted paneling and pediment detail above the fireplace, has the feel of an English clubroom. It is a perfect size for a more intimate gathering of friends or family.

Foyer

The floor plan allows for good circular flow through the entire first floor. This is especially true for the rooms at the rear of the house that are unified by the loggia located across the back of the property. Elegant limestone columns line the loggia and set the tone for a perfect space for outdoor dining. Guests can enjoy covered dining while they look onto the pool and its decorative candlelit lanterns.

Dining Room

Painting by Thomas Sully

Mantle Detail

French doors to loggia

Living room

Kitchen looking towards Family room

Master bedroom

Master bathroom

Pink bedroom

Green bedroom

Rear porch with flowers by Carmen Johnston, Nectar and Company

Limestone capital detail

Rear terrace and pool

LOTUS HOUSE

Deshpande House, Atlanta, Georgia 2004–2007

Warren Sirzyk Builder
See credits for individual designers

Flowers by Ed Castro Landscape, Atlanta, Georgia

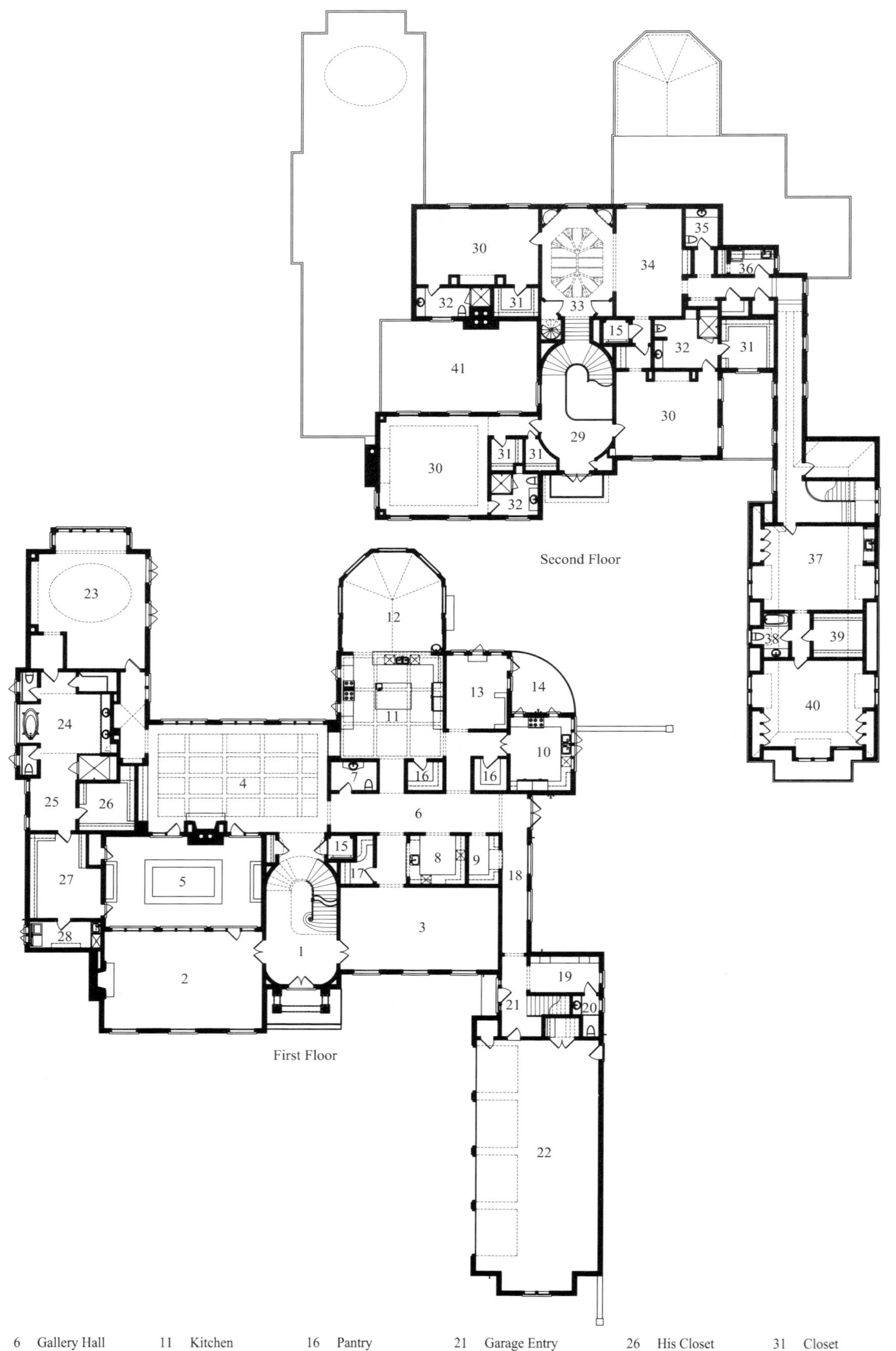

1 Foyer
2 Living Room
3 Dining Room
4 Family Room
5 Open Courtyard
6 Gallery Hall
7 Powder Room
8 Bar
9 Office
10 Caterer's Kitchen
11 Kitchen
12 Breakfast Room
13 Pooja Room
14 Open Terrace
15 Elevator
16 Pantry
17 China Closet
18 Hall
19 Mud Room
20 Half Bath
21 Garage Entry
22 Garage
23 Master Bedroom
24 Master Bath
25 Lady's Dressing Room
26 His Closet
27 Her Closet
28 Laundry Room
29 Upper Foyer
30 Bedroom
31 Closet
32 Bathroom
33 Atrium Room
34 Sitting Room
35 Half Bath
36 Upstairs Laundry
37 Staff Sitting Room
38 Staff Bath
39 Staff Closet
40 Staff Bedroom
41 Open To Below

Foyer by Cheryl Lucas and Jackie Fowler, Atlanta, Georgia

Living room by Barry Dixon, Washington, D.C.

Powder room by Cheryl Lucas and Jackie Fowler, Atlanta, Georgia

Houses should be a reflection of the interests or background of their owners. In this case the owners had deep roots in India. In choosing Regency-style architecture, the family was able to create a house connecting stylistically with the architecture of the Raj in India and also to architecture found in Georgia. In fact, both regions have histories of this style of architecture dating back to the 1830s. This sophisticated house with its white painted brick with limestone accents would appear appropriate in either India or Georgia.

Furthermore, the family was most generous to share their new home with the community by allowing the Atlanta Symphony Orchestra to use their house as the 2011 Decorator Show House. As such, the home was decorated by 29 of the country's top designers, who embraced the house's Indian theme in the most creative ways. Look carefully at the interiors and one can see elements of Indian design in many of the rooms, whether in the fabrics, furnishings, or architecture of the space.

The house is built around an interior garden courtyard with a lotus pond. This sunlit space is visible through steel casement doors from both the living and family rooms and serves as the heart of the home. Of special note is the family's meditation room, called a

Dining room by Turner Davis Interiors, Atlanta, Georgia

Family room by Patricia McLean Interiors, Atlanta, Georgia

Kitchen by Dillard Design Group, Atlanta, Georgia

Pooja room, which serves the family during its private devotion time.

To address the entertaining needs of the family, the house is designed for large groups of family and friends throughout the year. A variety of spaces were designed to create unique and special environments for these entertainments. On the first floor, the enclosed garden with its lotus pond provides a quiet retreat in the core of the house. Its steel casement doors open to the principal entertainment areas, giving good flow from room to room. On the lower level are the bar and recreation rooms, which open onto the covered open air porch for outside dining. This porch has a fireplace to warm the guests on cooler nights.

Breakfast room by Dillard Design Group, Atlanta, Georgia

Wet bar area by Scout for the Home, Atlanta, Georgia

But perhaps the most popular space is the roof top terrace, which can be reached by either a private elevator or by a winding stair. This roof terrace was reinforced with steel in anticipation of a large gathering of friends. The seating around its fireplace is the perfect place to sit at night to enjoy

Pooja room by Raymond Goins Designs, Atlanta, Georgia

Roof terrace by Boxwoods Gardens & Gifts, Atlanta, Georgia

Master bedroom by Meg Adams Interior Design, Atlanta, Georgia

a glass of wine and gaze up at the night sky. The view of the stars is one of the best in Atlanta as the house sits atop one of the highest points in the city and is located far enough from the glow of urban lights that the stars can be seen clearly.

Master bathroom by Meg Adams Interior Design

Master dressing room by Meg Adams Interior Design, Atlanta, Georgia

His and her closets by Peggy Snider-Houghton, Atlanta, Georgia

Upper stair hall by Katherine and William Tarleton Interiors, Atlanta, Georgia

Upstairs sitting room, Stan Topol and Associates, Atlanta, Georgia

Second-floor ladies' sitting area by Janie Hirsch Interior Design, Atlanta, Georgia

Bedroom by Janice Palmer and Manisha Kulkarn of Y Design International, Atlanta, Georgia

Second-floor study by McLaurin Interiors, Atlanta, Georgia

Lower-level Family room by Matthews Furniture Galleries and Design, Atlanta, Georgia

Van Cleef & Arpels
CAROLINA HERRERA

Game room by Brooke Merrill Home, Atlanta, Georgia

Terrace-level powder room by Habachy Designs, Atlanta, Georgia

Terrace-level bar by Barbara Heath of the Mercantile, Atlanta, Georgia

Terrace-level bar by Barbara Heath of the Mercantile, Atlanta, Georgia

Guest bedroom by Musso Design Group, Atlanta, Georgia

Potting room by Noelle Michael Interiors, Atlanta, Georgia

Overlook terrace by Barbara Heath of the Mercantile, Atlanta, Georgia

Let the Party Begin

Basketball Pavilion, Zionsville, Indiana, 2007–2008
R J Klein Builder
Interiors by Suzanne Kasler, Atlanta, Georgia

Overlooking a lake filled with geese and surrounded by forests and field, this pavilion originally began life as an enclosed basketball court for the son, an avid basketball fan. As the design evolved, the pavilion took on a larger purpose serving not only as a basketball and sports court, but also a venue for larger entertainments. The family has used the pavilion to stage corporate entertainment for the family's international guests, their daughter's wedding, family birthday parties, entertainment during the Indy 500 race, a barbecue before the Super Bowl in 2012, and fundraisers to support charitable causes around the

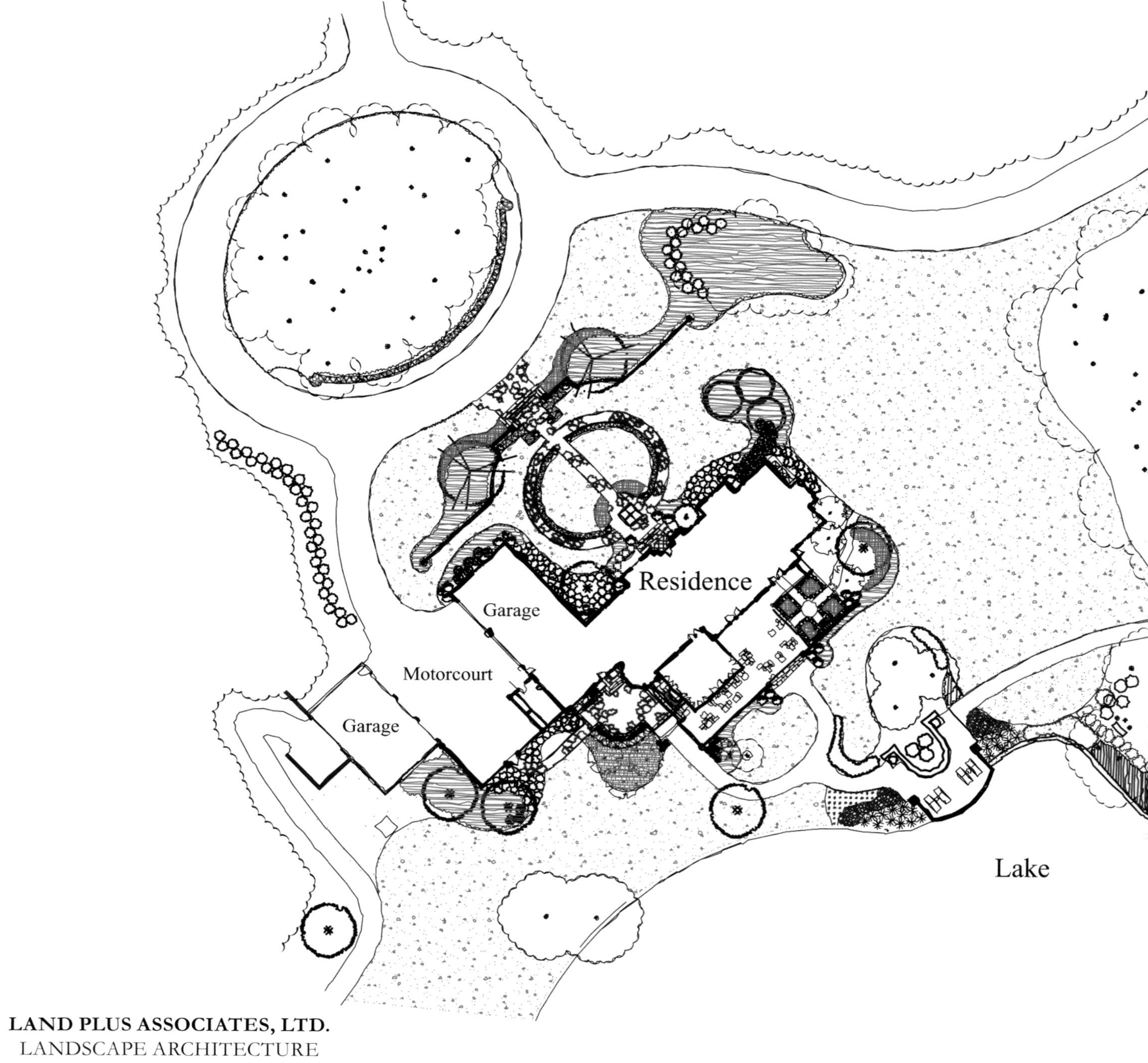

LAND PLUS ASSOCIATES, LTD.
LANDSCAPE ARCHITECTURE

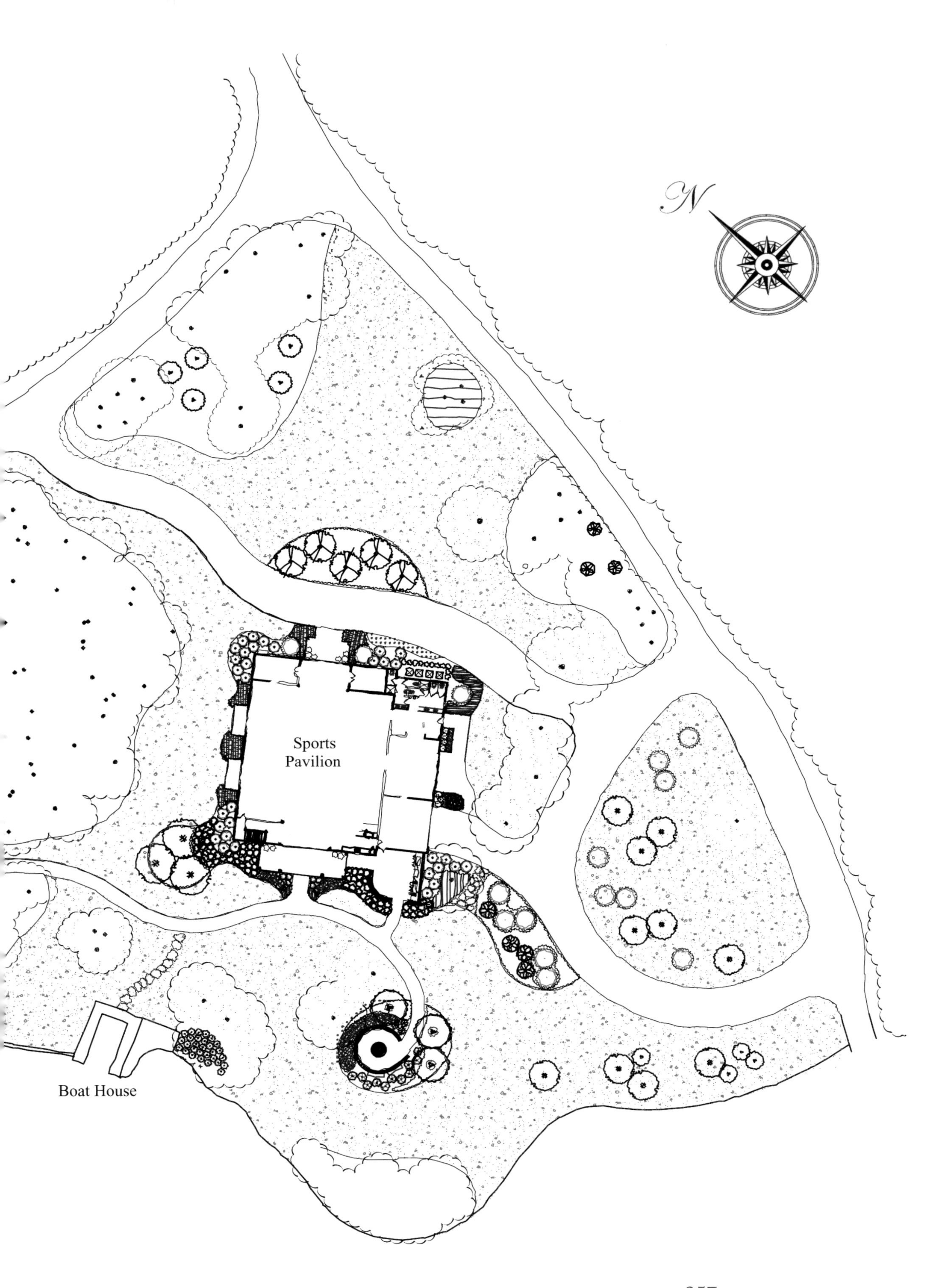
N
Sports
Pavilion
Boat House

world. The pavilion has created special memories and fun times.

The pavilion incorporates a regulation-size basketball court, a theater room, a full-size caterer's kitchen, men's and women's bathrooms, outdoor grilling area, and an upper balcony overlooking the court, which contains an English pub. Adjoining the pub is an open deck with a sunset view of the lake and its reed-lined edge. A fire pit located just off to the side of the pavilion is perfect for roasting marshmallows over an open fire on cool fall evenings.

Indoor basketball court

English pub on the upper balcony

Leather upholstered alcove seating

Theater room

Front elevation

CHATTAHOOCHEE LOW COUNTRY HOUSE

White House, Atlanta, Georgia, 2007–2009
Delaney Rossetti Contractors
Interiors by Amy D. Morris Interiors, Atlanta, Georgia

Occasionally a property presents unusual building challenges and this was the case for the future site of the White's home. The building site was located on a steep hillside with a rock outcropping overlooking a broad lawn located on a floodplain. The house was specifically designed to take advantage of this situation by arranging the first floor to open onto an upper rear terrace carved from the living rock. The lower terrace on the other side of the house opens onto the broad lawn.

The architecture captures the natural beauty of the land through its use of twin towers enclosing a long covered porch to capture the view across the lawn. One tower

Porch detail

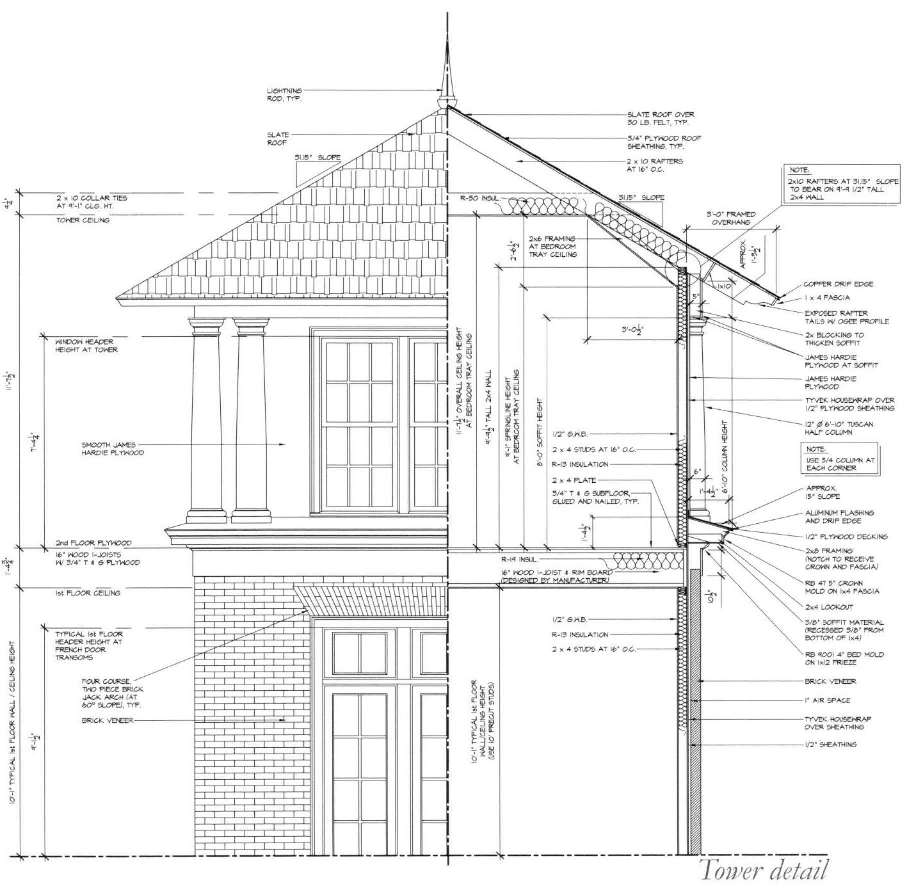

Tower detail

Lower terrace

contains the owner's heart-of-pine paneled study, while the other tower contains the master suite. The formal living room, dining room, and family room join these other rooms by opening directly onto the covered porch. This arrangement maximizes the views from each room and makes the porch the center of family activities while creating a good flow from room to room. The architectural detailing of the house takes its inspiration from the architecture of the Louisiana lowcountry. This

Foyer

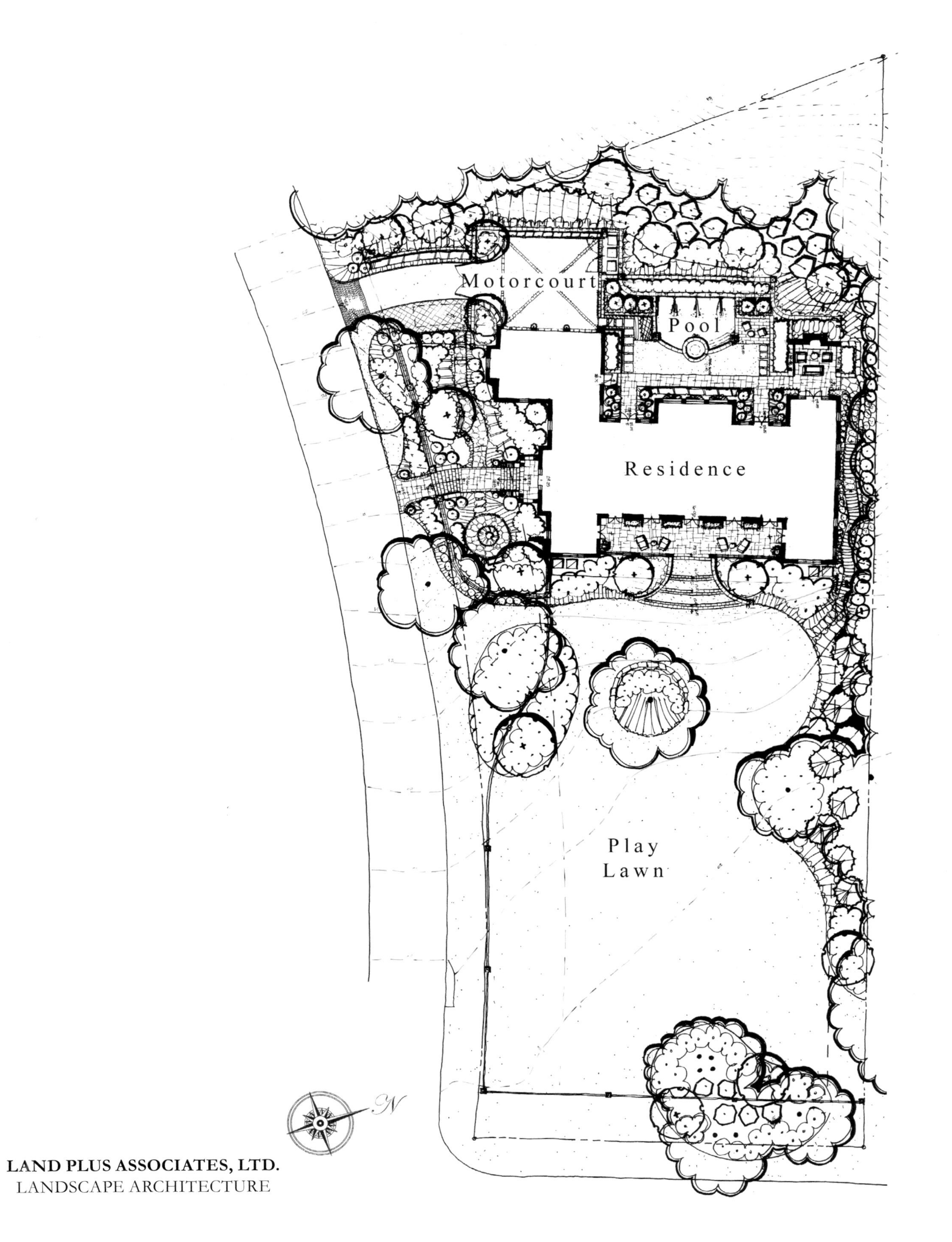

LAND PLUS ASSOCIATES, LTD.
LANDSCAPE ARCHITECTURE

Living room

Roots of Home
INSPIRED INTERIORS

is especially apparent on the porch, with its exposed rafters with decorative rafter tails and deep eaves, plank board ceiling, turned wood columns, simple picket railing, and stain-grade mahogany French doors with segmental transoms.

The interior finishes of herringbone brick floors and wood shiplap walls continue the theme. Anchoring the plan is the centrally located kitchen with its dramatic vaulted ceiling and beams. The first-floor master bedroom opens onto a covered porch of timber

Dining room

Family room

Kitchen

Rear hall

Mud bath

Study interior by Phoebe Howard Atlanta/Jacksonville

Master bedroom

Master bathroom

Daughter's bedroom

Upstairs craft room

Billiard room on lower level

The lower level bar opens to the covered porch

construction, which in turn adjoins the rear terrace. This master porch has built-in, electronically operated screen panels between the timber columns to provide year-round use of the porch. The pool, located on the

Lower level theater room

rear terrace, is placed against the decorative brick-and-stone rear retaining wall. The sound of water can be heard throughout the rear terrace area from the water feature built into the rear wall of the pool.

Rear terrace and pool